Now What?

Discovering Your New Life and Career After 50

James O. Armstrong

Lighthouse Publications, Inc.

Publisher
Lighthouse Publications
2028 Larkin Avenue
Elgin, IL 60123
(847) 697-6788
www.Lighthouse-Publications.com

Cover Design & Layout
Scott Wallis & Associates
2028 Larkin Avenue
Elgin, IL 60123
(847) 468-1457
www.ScottWallis.net

Dedication

T his book is dedicated to all of my fellow Baby Boomers and especially to my fellow classmates from the Webster Groves (Missouri) High School Class of 1965.

• Now What? •

Foreword

When I faced a career crisis not long ago I racked my brain wondering Now What? What next? How do I turn adversity into opportunity? Being understandably stressed and facing nothing but dead ends, I was fortunate enough to get this advice: "sometimes the biggest impediment to your success can be found between your ears."

That sounds a little harsh doesn't it? But I took it to be a challenge to have the courage to change and to have the faith that things will work out all right. Faith and courage certainly help, but I needed some examples, some real world examples with real people.

I wish I had this book then.

If you've picked up this book then you or someone you know is facing some harsh times and hard choices. You are lucky because my friend Jim Armstrong provides the examples that give the inspiration to help find the courage to change and to keep the faith that things will work out. This book is more than a book. It is a roadmap to new success for those of us facing professional upheaval and worse. The examples are real because they are about people just like you and me. They are inspiring because the people in this book got to the other side of the question "Now What?"

One inspiring person not profiled in this book is its author James O. Armstrong. Modesty prevents him from sharing his story, but I know Jim well enough to say that he has inspired others familiar with the professional and personal crises he has overcome – while still maintaining his good humor and faith. Jim's uplifting and inspiring book guides us, when faced with a seeming dead end in life, to draw upon faith to create the confidence to change.

This book is real because Jim, like others in this book, has himself answered the question "Now What?"

Read on and be inspired, too.

Keith G. Biondo
New York, NY

Contents

Preface

I f you just picked up a copy of this book wondering if you should buy it, you probably should. Here's why.

You just got laid off or downsized or right-sized at some large or mid-sized corporation in America, or you just decided to take that fabulous early-out package from your school district after 25 years on the job. Or, you are the spouse, friend or some other relative of someone where such a circumstance has just taken place. Or, you can see that it's a good idea to do some pre-planning or some contingency planning, in the event that some unforeseen circumstance takes place in the future.

That's why you're interested in buying this book. In fact, you just decided that it's a good idea to pick it up and pay for it at the cash register or to buy it online perhaps.

This book will not answer every question you have, nor will it resolve your every doubt about your own abilities in relationship to a future job.

But, this book will illustrate to you why there is hope for a brighter tomorrow. It will show you absolutely that you have a future, just as so many other men and women before you also had both a hope and a future, even after age 50. Your working life does not have to stop after age 50, 60, 70 or even 80. Nor does it especially matter what level of education you have had in the past. Nor does your region of the country relate to your current or future success in pursuit of the next open door in your career. Also, your race or religion doesn't have to correlate with your outcome either. Catholics, Protestants and Jews are all profiled, as well as an ardent environmentalist or two. Plus, men and women throughout the US are profiled, including blacks, whites and one Japanese-American.

In other words, this book quite literally profiles all of us in America, together with our hopes and dreams for a brighter tomorrow, despite the current circumstances we may be experiencing. Specifically, this book will provide you with a thumbnail portrait of 11 men and eight women all over age 50, and exactly what they are doing as well as how they happened to get to where they are today, be it their location, a specific job or a career path. This book will also provide you with a bird's eye view of some very promising future employment trends in America, which will be especially favorable to my generation of fellow baby-boomers.

It is my hope, as the author, that you will finish this book with a greater sense of hope for your own future than when you first began to read it. Obviously, I can only guarantee you just one outcome with certainty. If you choose not to make any sort of effort at all, then you will most definitely experience your own worst fear, namely that no one will want to hire you again. In other words, choosing not to act will most certainly become a self-fulfilling prophecy of the worst sort.

As Robert Frost, the talented New England poet, commented in his poem "The Road Not Taken": "Two roads diverged in a wood, and I – I took the one less traveled by, and that has made all the difference."

As the reader, your path still lies before you. So, make your next choice the best one you can possibly make.

Sincerely,

James O. Armstrong
Woodstock, Illinois

• Now What? •

Chapter One

• Now What? •

Introduction

What has fascinated us in life? It's the People section of Time Magazine, which became People Magazine. It's the Biography series on cable TV, which spawned Biography Magazine. It's also the front section each week of Parade magazine, where questions are asked and answers are provided about famous men and women.

I, too, confess that I have had a lifelong fascination with stories about people, which have included both the famous and the not so famous. For example, I remember reading nearly every biography in our grade school library at Avery School in Webster Groves, Missouri, where I grew up.

I also recall how much I loved the shorter versions of novels and the classics, which I encountered initially in my Classic Comic Books. As a young student, I literally collected the whole set, which had been written and produced at that time. Some of these treasures, I read over and over again.

Then, in college, I remember how I was especially fond of Cliff's Notes, particularly as a means of assisting me with an advanced French class at Westminster College in Fulton, Missouri.

As Americans, we appreciate a good story, especially one about a real person. And, we prefer those write-ups to come in smaller bites, if at all possible, because our time is limited and valuable.

The Over 50 Dilemma

For teachers and school administrators, it's typically 30 years and out. For others of us working at large and mid-sized companies, it's frequently a "sweetened offer," which causes us to accept an early retirement package.

Or conversely, we become a small cog in some endless series of corporate reorganizations or downsizing moves in our society. Often, sales just aren't there, and the company (which can even include law firms) simply needs to shed some people to save money. After all, there are certain economic realities in business.

But, all too often, the men and women being downsized just happen to be over 50. Sometimes, these people are 61 or 62 years old when they lose their "dream job."

As a person who is over the age of 50, we ask ourselves, what do we do next? Where do I go from here? Who will hire me? What company will add an over-50 employee?

How do I network? How do I write a resume, when I haven't done one in over 30 years? Do I really have to work for someone, as an employee, who's only half of my age? Is a home-office business viable for me?

In short, what are my options? Today, as never before in history, the oldest of our baby-boomers are now starting to ask these and similar questions. This book will address the answers, as we seek new directions for our lives.

And, Now, the Drum Roll...

Since you are reading this introduction, more than likely you are someone who has just experienced or you are about to experience a traumatic event in your job or career path. Or perhaps, you are the spouse or a close friend or counselor of someone, who is experiencing this loss/transition in their lives. Please understand that such events are common to men and women over age 50 in America. However, be assured that there is hope for each of us over 50, as we seek to reinvent ourselves. This statement applies to all of us, regardless of our education level, job, gender or race.

By way of introducing myself, please allow me to share with you that I understand these fears and hopes, as someone begins this process toward greater self-awareness and discovery. Why, you might ask? It is because during the 1990s I went through two corporate restructuring exercises, both of which left me without a job at different NYSE media companies. Both corporations had been excellent employers, just as I had been an excellent employee at the firms. Further, each of these assignments came to a close for similar reasons, which were each cited as a "reduction in force."

Of course, I appreciated the severance in each instance. I was also glad to receive some outplacement assistance in each case, as well. But, the day of reckoning finally does come, as these bridges end.

The good news is that life continues after your run in the large or mid-sized corporation, with the excellent fringe benefit package, or in your career as a nurse, teacher, minister, Wall Street executive, government worker or banker, for example.

During my professional life in the media sales industry, I have actually helped between 75 and 100 people find jobs of all sorts in different assignments and industries. I have also listened to the stories of a large number of men and women, who have completely reinvented themselves after age 50. Their examples are encouraging and true.

The purpose of this book is to share some of those insights with you from a selected group of men and women from all across America, from different walks of life, with a wide range in education and from different races. Their stories are unique and yet they are remarkable similar.

The good news in this book boils down to this observation: There is hope for each of us, as we reinvent ourselves after age 50. Yes, we can overcome discouragement. Yes, we can get past those initial feelings of loss. Yes, we can live to fight another battle on another day. Yes, there are still chapters in our lives, which are yet to be written. And, yes, perhaps the best actually does lie before us and not behind us.

Now is certainly the time to find out. It is my hope for you that this book will contribute to you in some measurable way, as you seek to reinvent yourself after age 50. Please let me know if this book helps you in some way.

· Now What? ·

Chapter Two

• Now What? •

Many Baby Boomers Will Work During Retirement

F or many of us, working will not be an option!

Let's say that you're 45 or 50 years old today. So, you haven't thought about it yet. But, you keep receiving those Social Security Administration print outs with regularity. Plus, you know you haven't saved much either.

Now, here's the shocker: You're in the majority! In fact, current statistics show that only 12% of Americans now have $250,000 or more in retirement savings. On the flip side of this equation, 88% of Americans haven't saved that much.

Please note: These Fast Facts from EBRI related to workers, who are age 25 and older, and their reported savings and investments, not including the value of their primary residence or defined retirement plan. Additional information about this report and related subjects is available at www.ebri.org, which is an independent nonprofit organization committed exclusively to data dissemination, policy research and education on economic security and employee benefits.

If you are someone who's fortunate enough to have worked for the federal, state or local government or for a local school district, good for you! Or, if you happen to still be working for a large or mid-sized corporation, which provides a pension to every employee, you have also been blessed more than you realize. In each of these scenarios, your total monthly cash flow in your retirement years will be greater than many, if not most of your friends, who are your age.

But, if you don't fall into such a category, where pension(s) will add to your monthly cash flow, then a good starting point in analyzing where you currently stand will be to discover the sum total of your savings, including all stock and bond portfolio values, any IRA or 401K amounts, plus CDs in the bank and regular passbook savings accounts in a bank, savings and loan or credit union. These in turn need to be added together to arrive at your total savings amount.

Next, simply multiply that figure times 5% for your yearly cash flow projection, based upon a more conservative stock and bond performance figure, according to Kevin Lang, who is a CPA with Lang & Becker. Specifically, you can expect $5,000 per year in income from $100,000 in savings and double that figure for $200,000 in savings. But, you should only count on $2,500 per year from $50,000 in total savings, based upon this formula.

So, what can we conclude? Well, the real shocker to my fellow baby boomers, as age 65 (and soon it will go up to age 66 for full retirement benefits from Social Security) draws ever closer, is that many of us will need to work, assuming that our health allows us to do so. Why?

Because dividends plus interest each year on our savings plus Social Security will not equal enough monthly cash flow for many if not most of us, as we age.

So, the very next time you receive a print out from the Social Security Administration, save it. Also, begin now to save more from each current paycheck, as you spend less overall between now and then (whenever that time will be).

In conclusion, working will not always be an option for us past age 65, 66 or 67, when we begin to receive full benefits from Social Security and cheaper health insurance from Medicare. The simple reason for many of us is that we will need the "extra" money from a job to help us pay our bills.

But, Some Baby Boomers Won't Work During Retirement

F or some of us, working will be just one more option!

As we look at every asset we own, we certainly need to include the current value of our home, less any loan(s) against it. Those loans need to include all of the following: (1) our basic home loan, (2) any home equity loan or second mortgage or (3) a reverse mortgage, even one that does not require a formal loan repayment each month or ever. Further, if we are fortunate enough to own a second or even a third home, we likewise need to take into consideration the equity position (i.e. the home's assessed value; any loan against it) of this home too.

Surprisingly, even without the value of our primary residence figured into this equation, today a record number of men and women have recently entered into what was once a rarified $1 million net worth category. In fact, according to the Spectrem Group, which is a Chicago-based consulting firm specializing in the affluent and retirement markets, a record of 8.3 million American households now have a net worth of $1 million or more. Furthermore, their survey found that 930,000 American households now have $5 million or more (Source: 2006 Spectrem Group Survey; please note that the net worth figures from this research excluded the value of someone's primary residence.)

Also, because three of my friends and acquaintances have lost both of their parents in recent years, still another factor has begun to enter into the overall picture for our baby boom generation. Specifically, current or future inheritance will not be an insignificant factor for a growing number of men and women in our age group. Why? Because homes and other real estate assets (and businesses) in our parents' generation have skyrocketed in value together with stock and bond portfolios in recent years. In fact, trillions of dollars will eventually change hands from one generation to the next over the next 20 years, from what Tom Brokaw earlier labeled as the "Greatest Generation" of World War II vets, as well as some Korean War-era vets to their children, who are today's baby boomers.

This factor by itself cannot nor should it be minimized in relationship to the future financial well-being of today's baby boomers, as the vanguard of this age group begins to approach an age 66 or 67 retirement point.

With all of these factors taken into consideration, a 2004 AARP Public Policy Institute Survey estimated that the average baby boomer born between 1946 and 1955 will actually have accumulated a total wealth of $859,000 at age 67. Further, the average baby boomer born between 1956 and 1965 will have $839,000 at 67, this study concluded. However, both of those totals surpass the wealth of today's 67 year old, who has an average of $560,000 (Source: 2004 AARP Public Policy Institute Survey).

Of course, with the advancement in quality health care for America's seniors, more of us as baby boomers will live longer and, in fact, 25% of us will make it to age 97, according to the National Center for Health Statistics.

But, our current and future career choices, among other decisions for our age group, will in part, stem from our financial well-being. In other words, the more money we ultimately have in the bank, the greater number of choices each of us will have in our golden years.

• Now What? •

Chapter Three

• Now What? •

Dr. James Sefrit

Retired School Administrator, Rides Again

Yesterday, his fourth grandchild was born. Who could ever have predicted that this is where Dr. James Sefrit would be in his life at age 56? Yet, here he was at St. Joseph's Hospital in St. Charles, Missouri welcoming into the world the newest addition to the Sefrit family. How proud grandpa was and also how relieved he was that both baby James Evan Sefrit and mom were doing just fine.

What a long journey it had been for that small town jock from Kirksville, Missouri until today, Jim thought. Along the way, he got to play football, basketball and baseball in high school and even received a professional baseball contract offer; he met and married his college sweetheart, who came from suburban Chicago, worked briefly for Southwestern Bell Telephone in a management training program, moved to St. Louis County, Missouri, and then worked during his career in teaching and high school administration for the next 31 years.

Retiring a year ago as one of the principals for Parkway North High School in suburban St. Louis, Dr. Sefrit had considered his options. Initially, of course, the thought occurred to him that he hadn't really made a full court press to find a "new" job in a really long time, to say the least. So, what were his choices? Where would he go? Who would he talk with? Or, did he really want to play golf every day, like one of his retired teacher/principal friends from the neighborhood?

Of course, with over 3 million teachers and school administrators in America today, all of these men and women will one day be asking the same or related questions that Dr. Sefrit asked a year ago.

In fact, not one drop of the champagne at his retirement party had even been poured before the offers began to roll into the Sefrit house. Would he like to do this? Would he consider doing that? Had he evaluated this option? Would Dr. Sefrit consider filling a slot at another Parkway High School for one semester as one of the principals now that he was "officially retired?" In other words, would Dr. Jim consider doing essentially what he had been doing elsewhere for just one semester?

At this point Sefrit sat down to evaluate and pray about all of his options– which were many. Certainly, he was grateful for all of the choices that had come across his desk. He was also a little surprised by the number of offers and the breadth of possibilities that they represented. Here is where someone's network of friends and allies in the profession paid off. Many individuals from teaching in the area knew Dr. Sefrit and, more importantly, they were aware that he had done a great job in his role as a principal of Parkway North High School.

Sometimes we wonder if anyone else is really watching us and our performance. We also find ourselves asking if anyone really cares whether or not I do a "good job." Of course, the real answer is that many individuals are watching more closely than we might think at the time. Furthermore, an excellent performance in our job will always be recognized in the long run. If no one else cares, others around us will see to it that the appropriate people know at "the right time." In other words, these fellow workers will themselves be the ones who make future hiring decisions.

So, in this early period of shortages of qualified teachers and school administrators, which our nation is already experiencing and will increasingly face in the future, Dr. Jim Sefrit provided a ready replacement during the first semester of school immediately after his "official retirement" in his former school district. And how glad they were to have someone as experienced as Dr. Jim last year.

Of course, at the same time, Sefrit has continued to teach graduate school courses in Educational Research, Curriculum and Administration Supervision part-time at Lindenwood University. In addition, he continued to supervise student teachers.

At the end of that first semester, immediately after his "official retirement," the next question was what to do now at this part of his journey? But, once again, Dr. Jim didn't need to wait long. One of the next round of choices available to Jim related to calling on a certain number of assigned school districts, primarily in St. Louis and other surrounding areas in Missouri. His newest employer wanted him to convince districts first and, then, their students to attend summer school classes in a curriculum provided by Newton Learning. As a part of the student presentations, boys and girls could even qualify for a whole range of great prizes, such as an electronic scooter or portable DVD player, just for signing up. Plus, every student who attended every day also got a $100 prize just for coming to class. The students were excited and Jim's first real foray into sales turned out to be a hit, both for the company and for him.

This experience also proved to be an exciting one for Sefrit himself, as he met a lot of new people and learned some new skills along the way.

So far, he hasn't even had the time to set up the educational consulting practice, which he at first had envisioned. The reason has been that he has simply been, in his words, "too busy" to do it. Plus, during the past year, Dr. James Sefrit has actually earned 60 percent more during retirement, in part because of his excellent pension program from the teaching profession, than he had previously made as a high school principal immediately before his retirement.

Dr. James Sefrit currently serves as senior high school principal at
Westminster Christian Academy in Ladue, Mo.

The good news for all of us is this: We don't
automatically have to make less money after retirement than
we previously made. Also, it's a pleasant surprise to find out
that there will always be openings for qualified people, who
have something to contribute to our society.

• Now What? •

Linda Krinop

B&B Proprietor, Loved People

Welcome to the Victorian Garden in Osgood, Indiana (Population: 1600) where Linda Krinop is the owner and bed & breakfast proprietor together with her husband Paul.

Specifically, just before her 50th birthday, Linda took the plunge into a very different line of work than this Ohio-born, high school graduate had ever previously experienced. She and her husband had stayed at a number of B&Bs over the years, but, increasingly, Linda had often commented to Paul that "if she were the owner of this B&B," she would do things a little differently. Finally, Paul told her, "Why don't you just start one?"

And, that's exactly what Linda did.

Before 1995, when she opened her very own B&B, Linda Krinop had been the owner of two different flower shops and she also served as a dental assistant and x-ray technician. Additionally, she was a book keeper and, originally, the secretary in the Engineering Department of Cincinnati, Inc., where she met her husband.

Why has this career choice worked out so well and why will it continue to work out well for Linda in the future, you might ask? First, Linda's husband Paul is now close to retirement– he will turn 61 next year. By taking a somewhat early retirement, his company will then pay for half of his health insurance premium until this couple qualifies for Medicare, thereby taking a huge load off of Linda and her husband in terms of what this expense will cost their family. Second, Linda enjoys working in her home, which not everyone does. Third, their daughter Tracy, their son-in-law Calvin and grandson, Xavier Gunner Simpson, moved back to the area from New York City. Therefore, as an important, other caregiver in the family, Linda now has access to her grandson almost any time she wants to see him and watch him for her daughter. Linda's daughter works as an RN, while her son-in-law Calvin serves as a Supervisor for Kraft Foods, which was generous enough to pay for his MBA in Business Administration in return for working for the company an additional two years. Finally, Linda likes to cook and does an excellent job. Those exotic recipes, which some of us enjoy reading about in a publication like Gourmet Magazine, Linda actually creates and serves to her guests as part of her overall hospitality package at The Victorian Garden.

During the past year, Paul Krinop, Linda's husband, had "a close call" during his recovery process from knee replacement surgery. Specifically, Paul's home healthcare nurse after his operation thought that he might be experiencing a blood clot, which turned out to be a correct diagnosis. After moving to a nearby hospital in Batesville, Indiana, Paul was transferred up to Cincinnati, where he received excellent care in helping him to get rid of a blood clot in his lungs. The Coumadin blood thinner worked out and, now, he has returned back to his job and feels nearly 100% again just five months later.

For her part, Linda regrets that she didn't take this step to become a B&B owner/proprietor 10 years earlier. Of course, she thought that most people would never come to a tiny community such as Osgood, Indiana, but that simply was not the case. On the Monday after my wife and I recently left her home and B&B, Krinop confided that two couples from

33

France were both visiting the area and staying at her B&B. Of course, Versailles is one of the nearby communities and there is also a noticeable French influence overall in this part of Indiana. In addition, Krinop has hosted men and women and whole families from Canada and Mexico, as well as those from California, Maine and many other points both near and far on the compass, she said.

How did she and Paul get together? Here's how that happened. Linda had been working as a secretary in the engineering department of the same company, where Paul worked as a draftsman. At first, Paul rejected the suggestion of a mutual friend to take Linda out since the two of them worked together. But, Paul's male friend persisted with the suggestion of inviting her to a Valentine's Day dance in Osgood in 1968. At the end of their very first date, Paul looked at Linda and he announced to her that he was going to marry her. To herself, if not out loud, Linda said, "Yeah, right." But, by April 4, 1968, the two of them were engaged and by December 7, 1968, they had indeed tied the knot. Paul's words, if not prophetic, were clearly right.

For its part, The Victorian Garden (www.bbonline.com/in/victorian) is like taking a step back into our Victorian past in the US. Going back into a moment almost frozen in time, visitors will step into the foyer of a neat home out of yesterday, which is complete with its rich woods, Postmaster's desk in the living room and inviting downstairs decor. Going up the golden oak staircase, guests will experience lighting fixtures out of yesteryear plus lace curtains, which remind us all of days gone by. In fact, there is even a wonderful gazebo outside in the Victorian Garden itself. With a wide variety of plants outside and pictures of grandma and grandpa inside on the walls of this B&B, the whole picture becomes nearly complete.

The Victorian Garden, which was built in 1895 near Downtown Osgood, still has its original oak woodwork, pocket doors in such places as the parlor, the original fireplace downstairs for additional embellishment and pleasure for the weary traveler.

The visitor has three spacious rooms from which to choose. Each has cable TV and air conditioning, with a unique theme and special antiques. Single occupancy ranges from $65/night, with double occupancy ranging from $85-$95/night, which includes breakfast the next morning. Be prepared to experience a delicious presentation the next morning at no additional charge. By the way, this Christian couple, who are members of the local Methodist church, also offer a minister discount. So, don't be afraid to ask for it, if this discount applies to you or to your family.

Today, life is great in Osgood, particularly at The Victorian Garden. Just ask Linda and Paul Krinop, the owners and proprietors.

• Now What? •

Chapter Four

• Now What? •

Clarence O. Williamson

IRS Role Agent, Offers Financial Advice

Although born in New York City on August 15, 1946, Clarence O. Williamson Jr. moved to Greensboro, North Carolina with his parents, when he was only nine weeks old. There, his father took advantage of the GI Bill to complete college at A&T College in Greensboro. Upon graduation, instead of moving back to New York City, as earlier planned, Clarence's dad found a job in Greensboro and the family stayed put.

Williamson himself, an African-American, went through the Greensboro Public Schools, where he graduated from high school in 1964. Interestingly, his graduating class was actually the last totally segregated high school class in Greensboro, N.C. In college, Clarence graduated from Lincoln University, which is located in Lincoln University, Pennsylvania in 1968.

His employment after graduation ranged from working as a marketing researcher and a distillery representative in New

York and New Jersey for Seagram Distillers, to serving as a sales representative in various territories for Xerox Corporation in Connecticut, to working as a stock broker for Merrill Lynch also in Connecticut. Then, Clarence's career began to take a different turn, as he went to work at the New York Stock Exchange. There he served in various middle management positions for the exchange.

Along the way, Clarence O. Williamson – a.k.a. C.O. – also attended graduate schools at Temple School of Law in Philadelphia and New York School of Finance in New York City, located near Wall Street.

Next, he went to work for McGraw Hill's *BusinessWeek* magazine in a St. Louis-based area, where he served in a circulation development role that targeted large companies and trade associations. Also, at that time, he applied and was admitted to graduate school at Washington University's Olin School of Business, where he received his MBA in Business in 1986. Initially, at least, because of his job at McGraw Hill, he received a maximum amount of tuition reimbursement during his first year of graduate school.

But, the draw of North Carolina and his family there remained strong for this executive, and, so he returned to his boyhood home town of Greensboro, North Carolina, where he initially sold life insurance for Life of Virginia.

Where does Clarence O. Williamson Jr. work and live today and what are his current duties and responsibilities?

Approximately 13 years ago, Williamson founded TWC Financial, a firm that prepares taxes and represents its clients before the Internal Revenue Service throughout the U.S. In fact, after three tries, Clarence finally passed all four parts of the IRS examination for Enrolled Agent. The IRS actually decides how many people it will accept into this position each year to represent individuals and companies before it in terms of a wide range of tax issues. An enrolled agent, as Clarence explained, is enrolled to practice before the IRS in all tax related matters, such as trust funds, the amount of taxes owed, business taxes and other related issues. To maintain his enrolled agent credentials, he actually attends 50-70 hours per year for continuing education in the field.

During tax preparation season, C.O. needs approximately 12 employees, while his staff shrinks considerably after that time each year. Most of these employees actually work on a commission basis in this part of his business, which is seasonal. But, the representation side of his practice goes on all year. For businesses and for individuals, who file each quarter, Clarence maintains a staff CPA, with a master's degree in accounting, plus two MBAs with a concentration in Accounting.

So, how did Clarence re-invent himself? Well, he emerged as an entrepreneur in the tax preparation and tax representation arena right back where he started his life in Greensboro, North Carolina. For Williamson, the obvious conclusion relates to the absolute certainty in life of death and taxes. With the ever increasing complexity of taxes in America, the necessity for tax payers to utilize the services of someone, like Clarence O. Williamson, Jr., appears self evident.

Today, C.O. remains single, although a number of women at his mother's church keep expressing an interest in him. But, Williamson admits that he has become content the way he is plus, he added, he's also moody. In his company, he has decided not to expand because he wants to maintain a high level of quality in his operation. Also, Clarence's mother, who has recently experienced some medical problems, lives with him.

Williamson, a loving family man, today has hired a cook, who makes such gourmet dishes for dinner as red snapper, with crab stuffing. He admits that eating well has become much more important these days. C.O. appreciates good jazz, too, and has become a fan of XM radio. And, although he owns a great set of golf clubs, it's actually been several years since he's played a round. He still reads *BusinessWeek* and *Fortune* magazine on a regular basis.

And, he calls North Carolina his home.

Lyn Carlson

Nurse, Turned Flight Instruction School Owner/Pilot Extraordinaire

O n a recent Sunday afternoon, this writer caught up with a successful female business owner, whose flight instruction and general aviation business is physically located at John Wayne Airport in Orange County, California. But how did Evelyn A. Carlson, a Nursing Instructor at St. John College in Cleveland, Ohio, ultimately emerge as a partner in a Learn to Fly business on the West Coast and become a pilot extraordinaire? Here's the story.

As an intermediate step, Carlson began to teach both nursing and flight instruction as an Assistant Professor in two different departments at Kent State University, one of which was Technology (think Flying). Lyn commented that both of these teaching endeavors were not so different as they might seem at first glance. Sure, the data itself was different, but not the process. Both had scientific and technical aspects; each involved manipulating equipment and both, at times, required instantaneous decisions.

Of course, as we age and experience a wide range of different life circumstances, a number of unexpected choices emerge. Just ask Lyn Carlson if that didn't happen to her. Furthermore, some of the chapters in our lives take place before age 50, while other parts of our life evolve later.

Along the way, Lyn served in the Peace Corps in Nyeri, Kenya, where she taught nursing. Also, during graduate school, Carlson received a National Institute of Health full scholarship and living expenses stipend. In 1974, Lyn completed her MSN from Case Western Reserve University in Ohio. After completion of her Master's degree, she initially began teaching nursing at the baccalaureate level. But, then, her love for flying plus her advanced degree combined to also allow her to teach flying in Kent, Ohio, too. At the time, Lyn was 35 years old.

For the next four years, Lyn arrived at the airport early in the morning, where she served as the flying instructor from 7 AM until Noon. Then, she would teach nursing in the afternoon. Finally, she would drive back to the School of Technology building on campus at the end of the day to serve as an assistant professor in Technology, where she taught the evening ground schools until 9 or 10 PM. What a schedule this dedicated teacher and flight instructor kept in those days.

As a pilot, she joined the Aircraft Owners and Pilots Association (AOPA) in 1979 as member #006905147. During 1981, Lyn won the Amelia Earhart Medal by finishing in first place in one of the events at the National Intercollegiate Flying Association meet, which was held at the University of North Dakota. By 1982, Carlson was already listed in the Who's Who of American Women.

In her case, the circumstance, which led Lyn to move back to California "right back where she started" went like this. Due to the declining health of her grandparents, who held a special place in Lyn's heart, she returned to the Golden State to spend time with them and help care for them. Back in California, Carlson also began to hand out resumes and, ultimately, wound up as Chief Flight Instructor at Sunrise Aviation in Santa Ana, California. So, she stayed in Southern California, where her family had long established ties, which actually went back four generations.

After joining the team at Sunrise as partner and Certified Flight Instructor (CFI), Lyn helped to develop FAA Approved Flight Training Programs, which included the writing of ground and flight training syllabi, as well as getting them approved by the FAA. She also supervised the training given by more than 25 other flight instructors. As Chief Instructor, she was ultimately responsible for certifying all student school records for accuracy and compliance. She also gave flight instruction herself and was responsible for Stage Checks.

Of course, Carlson was also a strong influence on the growth at Sunrise Aviation from just two smaller, single-engine aircraft at the outset to its 32 aircraft plus 25 flight instructors today. Raised originally in Redwood City, California, Lyn spent every summer in Newport Beach. Like her parents, she too attended UCLA, where she earned her undergraduate degree in Nursing.

In her late 40s, Lyn actually flew solo across the Atlantic in a Rockwell 114 from El Monte, California to Guernsey, Channel Islands via Lakeland, Florida (where she stopped for tanking) to Gander, Newfoundland and Santa Maria in the Azores. Why had Carlson taken such a bold step? As a pilot, she was intent on getting everything possible out of her lifetime flying experience. This goal on her part made the trip inevitable.

Obviously, upon her return from this adventure, she became highly in demand as a speaker before local 99s in her area. The Ninety-Nines organization, which was founded in 1929 by 99 women pilots, existed then and now for the mutual support of its members. Not surprisingly, Amelia Earhart became the first president of one of these local groups in her area. During 1992 and 1993, Lyn continued to make additional motivational talks about flying solo across the Atlantic, while she also engaged in one-on-one teaching for men and women, who were considering the same type of flight.

Of special note, during 1995, Lyn Carlson was also chosen for the prestigious FAA National Flight Instructor of the Year Award. Winning at the local and regional FAA levels, the national selection committee was made up of representatives from all the major General Aviation organizations, which included the Aircraft Owners and Pilots Association, the National Business Aircraft Association, the National Association of Flight Instructors, the General Aviation Manufacturers Association and the Experimental Aircraft Association in addition to officials from the FAA itself. In fact, the entire process actually took four months to complete. What an honor for Lyn Carlson!

By 1998, Carlson had also added the additional title of Director of Training at Sunrise Aviation because her job duties and responsibilities also included student enrollment. Furthermore, from 1995 until the present, Lyn has also administered the FAA computer knowledge exams in her area.

In addition, Lyn Carlson has also had the distinction of serving in each of the following capacities, which have included being a National Transportation Safety Board Consulted Party (during 1997-1998). In this instance, for example, Carlson reviewed data associated with a fatal student accident and wrote an official party report, which was included in the final accident write-up. Then, as an AOPA Flight Instructor Refresher Clinic Lecturer from 1997 until 2003, Lyn traveled throughout the US to present and discuss topics required by the FAA. One such topic was an in-depth review of 14 CFR Part 61: Certification for Pilots and Instructors. For its part, the Aircraft Owners and Pilots Association is one organization authorized by the FAA to offer the required 16-hour Flight Instructor refresher courses needed to renew someone's Flight Instructor Certificate. She also continues to serve as a Designated Pilot Examiner. In this capacity, Carlson gives Pilot Practical Tests for Private, Instrument and Commercial candidates (in airplanes). The examination, in this instance, includes both an oral and an in-flight practical test. The DPE position actually represents an appointment by the FAA and, as such, is considered a prestigious one in the flying community. While the FAA does give these tests, staffing does not permit them to do the majority of Practical Exam flights at the General Aviation level. Therefore, DPEs are designated by the FAA to examine for proficiency to determine who gets pilot certificates in many instances.

Dedicated nurse, teacher, college professor, flight instructor and trainer, Lyn Carlson has today returned to her home state of California to do what she really loves and what all of the experiences in her life have prepared her to do: teach and fly herself. Most of us cannot do either. But, for those of us who live in Southern California, who desire to learn to fly, Lyn Carlson and her company would be a great place to start.

After all, as Cessna used to comment in its ads of yesterday, "If I can fly, you can fly."

Chapter Five

• Now What? •

Beber Helburn

UT Professor, Turned Arbitrator-Mediator

On a recent Southwest Airlines flight from Dallas to Oklahoma City, I happened to meet an individual who specializes in a very distinct field. As he explained, his responsibility comes into practice in situations when there is a dispute between a labor union and management that cannot be resolved by the parties themselves. Yes, he belongs to an elite group of men and women in the U.S., who are called into play only when labor arbitration is required. Arbitration in the U.S. is voluntary in the private sector and mandated in the federal sector, but the parties don't need to go through the federal government and often don't decide on an arbitrator.

Further, at age 65, he too definitely reinvented himself from a University of Texas Graduate Business School professor to what he is today, a U.S. labor arbitrator-mediator. After nearly 30 years at the University of Texas at Austin, I. B. "Beber" Helburn went from teaching Labor Relations, HR Management, Negotiation and Arbitration,

51

with a part-time job of serving in his current capacity, to now practicing what he had preached full-time.

Of course, since Beber Helburn had begun his University of Texas at Austin Business School stint in January, 1968, UT Austin has steadily risen in prominence to what it has become today. Modestly, Helburn doesn't choose to take any particular credit for the school's current reputation, although, in all honesty, being able to take classes from such a professor would be exciting for any student.

After completing his Ph.D from the University of Wisconsin Industrial Relations Institute with a major in Industrial Relations, Dr. Helburn principally served as a university professor, but he also briefly functioned as a consultant to the Committee on Wages and Employment to the House of Representatives in Texas for approximately one year (which reportedly led to the passage of the first state minimum wage law). Helburn has been listed on the Federal Mediation and Conciliation Service's labor arbitration panel from 1972 until the present, the labor panel of the American Arbitration Association since 1974, and the labor panel of the National Mediation Board since 1992.

Helburn has been involved with Arbitration panels over the years, which have included all of the following companies: AT&T and the Communications Workers of America; Continental Airlines and the International Association of Machinists (Flight Attendants); Continental Airlines and the Air Line Pilots Association (ALPA);

Federal Express Corporation and ALPA; GAF Corporation and PACE International Union; Internal Revenue Service and the National Treasury Employees Union; International Paper Company and PACE plus the IBEW; Lone Star Steel and the United Steelworkers of America; Lucent Technologies and the Communications Workers of America; Major League Baseball and the Major League Players Association (Salary); Southwest Airlines and the International Association of Machinists (Reservation Agents); Southwest Airlines and TWU Local 555 (Ramp Personnel); U.S. Customs Service and the National Treasury Employees Union; U.S. Postal Service and the American Postal Workers Union, National Association of Letter Carriers and the National Rural Letter Carriers' Association; and the Veterans Administration Medical Center and the AFGE Local 1633.

On the day we met he was flying to Oklahoma City and, then, driving to Elk City, Oklahoma in order to arbitrate a dispute between the US Postal Service and the American Postal Workers Union over a staffing issue. In fact, Helburn has often arbitrated contract interpretation and discipline issues in the past at many other US Post offices in the southwest and southeast, as he has also done at Federal Express and Southwest Airlines too, among others.

For Beber, his typical Tuesday-Thursday weekly schedule now does not represent as much "a reinvention as more of an evolution," he said. As an exception, he

53

commented that he was willing to take a Southwest Airlines case on Monday because, unlike many clients, Southwest Airlines and its unions are willing to set cases for Monday hearings. Furthermore, he sometimes, but not always, works long hours to get disputes resolved. Please bear in mind that before his "official" retirement from UT Austin, he was certainly able to pepper his Graduate B-school lectures with many real world examples that sometimes were "stranger than fiction" as he concluded.

Today, Helburn may hear two or even three cases, each in a different location, and maybe each in a different state, in the course of a week. This labor arbitrator currently experiences a 50-55% settlement rate, before the parties get to Beber. Often, he said just the threat of an imposed resolution rather than a voluntary settlement motivates the conflicting parties to reach an agreement before meeting with him.

In fact, a tactic that he often uses in these situations goes something like this. Before beginning the hearing, Helburn will tell the opposing parties that perhaps they should each "take one last shot at it" in an attempt to reach a settlement that both sides can accept. In fact, he told me that this tactic, by itself, periodically results in a settlement.

When he's not dealing with arbitration matters, Helburn stays involved as the co-chair of a $10.5 million capital campaign for Congregation Beth Israel in Austin, Texas. Others have served more total times as president than he has, but he is the only one in the congregation's 128 year history to have served two separate terms – 10 years apart – as president.

Helburn, who turned 65 in August of 2003 now qualifies for Medicare plus he and his wife Judith, whom he met on the first day of freshman English at the University of Wisconsin-Madison, also continue to receive medical coverage through his university group health insurance plan. Beber and Judith have two married children and four grandchildren living nearby. Judith is a Certified Sageing Leader for the Spiritual Eldering Institute. She has also been active in and on the board of Story Circle Network for Women with Stories to Tell, which has been organized as an international organization since 1998.

Over the years, this stalwart adopted Texan has written books and monographs such as "Public Employer-Employee Relations in Texas: Contemporary and Emerging Developments" (1971), he has contributed chapters and proceedings toward a better understanding within his profession and written articles for several professional journals and published teaching cases.

In conclusion, we should certainly realize that there will always be labor disputes, which will continue to provide valuable work for a seasoned professional like I. B. Beber Helburn. While not an employee, this independent contractor does perform a valuable function for our economy as a whole. Plus, he continues to be well compensated, too, for his time (including travel) and his skilled arbitration efforts.

Sheridan Yerk

Registered Nurse, Became Healthcare Industry Administrator

C onceived in a West Coast internment camp for Japanese Americans at the end of World War II, Sheridan Yerk was born in northwest Illinois in February 1946, three months after her mother and father moved to Marengo, Illinois. The second of four children, Sheri went on to graduate from high school there and, then, continued her education in nursing school at what is today Rush Presbyterian St. Luke's Hospital in Chicago. In March 2007, it will be 40 years since she graduated and became a registered nurse. The rest of Sheri's story focuses on someone who saw the mountain ahead of her and climbed it.

For 22 of the next 40 years, Yerk worked in various capacities at St. Anthony's Hospital in Rockford, Illinois, where she most frequently supervised an Intensive Care Unit in the hospital, among other duties and responsibilities. At the end of her time there, the hospital went through a downsizing exercise, where she and a number of other men and women experienced an all-too-predictable reduction in force. Her last assignment at St. Anthony's had been managing a post-anesthesia wing of the hospital. While she received a severance, which so many other men and women have also received, the real question for her and, by extension, for us is "How do I deal with this adversity?" When she met with a human resources representative from the hospital in the cafeteria to discuss her options, she told him that "she was a fortunate person," who was married and had a husband with a good job. In fact, she concluded in this interview, she had a lot more advantages than many people.

Of course, naturally she applied for unemployment insurance and received it for a short time. Because of her overall background and experience, she went up to Beloit, Wisconsin to check out a lower level position, but wound up interviewing for a director level position instead at Beloit Hospital. In the end, she ended up getting what was actually a better job with more benefits and higher pay. So, one possible outcome that can happen to anyone of us in a downsizing/rightsizing exercise in our lives might be an even better job than we used to have. A part of the outcome, as Sheri Yerk illustrates all too well, has to do with our attitude in life.

In getting from point A to point B in this circumstance, Sheri had to come against self-doubt and any feelings of being upset. Instead, like the 60-year-old Rocky from the recently released Rocky Balboa movie, she had to simply come out fighting and keep her head down, as she went forward during the tougher times of her life.

Having transferred to Mercy Health System based in Janesville, Wisconsin 14 years ago, Sheridan Yerk has undertaken a variety of different assignments, with an ever increasing level of responsibility. Initially, when she went over to Mercy, she was the director for the ICU, Special Care Unit/telemtry and Obstetrics. Then, Mercy started an Open Heart Program. But since that time, she has served as the clinic manager of a lab, radiology unit, surgery, outpatient and emergency clinics through the Mercy Health System in Southern Wisconsin, which today also includes a small rural hospital. She currently manages four such facilities for Mercy. Because of the issue of providing quality medical care in rural areas, Mercy does receive some federal funding for the hospital, which is under her wing. Her current responsibilities include interviewing applicants, hiring them and then also training her new hires at these facilities.

Mercy Health System, which today ranks as the #1 rated company in the US for Seniors to work according to the 2006 AARP Study, constantly stresses the type of continuous improvement in their procedures, which have been famous in the manufacturing sector in the US. Expansion at Mercy, she explained, is today dictated by the need for additional programs to be offered. Those programs, in turn, drive the architectural design; Mercy does not take a "build it and hope the patients will come" type of approach. Mercy

Health System also represents a great example where talent, in terms of promotions, dictates versus a college degree or advanced degree being used as the final qualifier.

Rounding out her life, Sheri has always put her family and its needs first. Married for 39 years to her husband Gary, she raised three sons and a daughter. And today she enjoys spending time with her eight grandchildren, the oldest of which is 16 and the youngest of which is now an infant. She and her husband still live today in Belvidere, Illinois, where they raised their children. In terms of her spouse, Sheri described an active involvement from her husband in bathing her children when they were young and interacting with them in ways that many husbands even today rarely do. Cooperation was the goal they constantly strived to attain at her home and, apparently, their efforts often succeeded. While Gary would work during the day, Sheridan would frequently work the evening shift so that one parent would always be there with their children during their time growing up at home.

Sheri Yerk also described taking time off from work to attend all sorts of sporting events for her four children. In fact, she commented that she rarely missed any of their games during their school years. Even today, most of Sheri's children live nearby and frequently see her for dinner on Sundays and even sometimes during the week. For Sheri and her family, flexibility was also a key to their success. Being accessible as a parent, especially right after school each day, also seems to have worked at the Yerk house in preparing her now grown up children to make good decisions later.

Sheridan's husband Gary, who has now been officially retired for the past three years from a heavy construction company, today helps out on a part-time basis at a trucking company where one of his sons works. In recent years, Sheri's husband has emerged as an excellent cook, who also knows how to shop at the grocery store, run errands for the family to the bank and perform other chores, while Sheri works each day. Adjustment throughout their marriage has meant a series of shifting duties and responsibilities at home for this successful couple. On the fun side of the ledger, one of the big loves in her family has been riding motorcycles and taking vacations to see family members, like a 90 year old aunt in the State of Washington.

Sheri and her husband are currently building an addition to their weekend lake house, which is located on White Sand Lake in Lac Du Flambeau, Wisconsin. They also own 70 acres in the northern part of Boone County, where she and other members of her family do trap shooting, fishing and enjoy family time together.

Her husband's mother, who is currently 86 years old, has lived with Sheri and her family for the past 29 years since she became a widow at the age of 45. Sheri's mother-in--law, who worked until she turned 65, has continued to remain active in her church as a part of the bell choir, despite the fact that she doesn't drive.

Raised as a Baptist, Sheri and her husband occasionally today attend the Catholic church near their home.

What was Sheridan Yerk's key to success? Flexibility, both on the job and at home. Plus, Sheri has always put her family first and she has been fortunate to be able to work in nursing initially and, later, in administration for organizations, which shared her values. In addition, because Sheri was so successful in terms of her bedside manner in the hospital, she was promoted into nursing supervision and ultimately into medical administration. Sheri's bottom-up success story says a lot about someone's hard work and what the rewards can still be in our country today. Her well-deserved achievements now also say that where someone started in life in no way determines where they will end up in our society. Her emphasis involves going on a family picnic or venturing out on a pontoon boat on a 1300 acre lake or simply spending time with her new grandchild.

That's Grandma Sheri's life today and it's a full one.

• Now What? •

Chapter Six

• Now What? •

Steven S. Plumb

Park Maintenance Consultant, Travels the U.S.

When I first met Steve Plumb, a Park Maintenance Consultant and an instructor for the National Playground Safety Institute, he was on a flight with me from Memphis to Chicago. He was flying to Chicago rather than to Colorado Springs, Colorado, which is the major airport nearest to his mountain home in Hartsel, Colorado located 80 miles away, because he was visiting his Chicago-based fiancé. She would soon marry him and move to Colorado as his wife.

Steve first met his wife at a parks and recreation workshop in Chicago. Mary was formerly employed by a variety of public park and recreation agencies, and now works as an administrative assistant for a construction company that specializes in public agency construction projects in the Chicagoland area. This couple had been friends for nearly 30 years and only recently did their relationship take another turn entirely, which resulted in an exciting conclusion that was far different than either one of them had previously imagined.

Today, Steve works part-time for Leon Younger & PROS, an organization that provides a wide variety of consulting services for public park and recreation agencies throughout the U.S. In essence, Leon Younger & PROS books Steve into his next assignment, almost like the fabled Paladin of Western lore from the early days of TV. However, the difference for this fast "gun for hire" relates to cleaning up maintenance problems in parks instead of a group of Western bad guys.

After graduating from Shawnee Mission West High School in 1964, Plumb went to Colorado State University in Ft. Collins, Colorado, where he earned his Bachelor of Science degree in Outdoor Recreation. After a two-year stint in the U.S. Army, he graduated from Pennsylvania State University in University Park, Pennsylvania in 1972 with a Master of Science in Park & Recreation Administration, with Minors in both Geography and Landscape Architecture. He then moved to Illinois and spent the next 31 years directing the park maintenance operations for two different Park Districts.

During one of the high points of his career, Steve served for two years as Interim Executive Director for the Elmhurst Park District in Elmhurst, Illinois, where he was responsible for a $10.4 million agency budget and managed 41 full-time and 400+ part-time and seasonal employees. In this capacity, he was responsible for developing and coordinating the 23-mile long Salt Creek Greenway Trail with nine other public agencies, among other duties and responsibilities. Officially retiring from the Elmhurst, Illinois Park District as Director of Park Services in September, 2002, Plumb has been traveling throughout the U.S. ever since teaching Certified Playground Safety Inspector courses, and completing maintenance consulting projects with men and women who do exactly what he used to do prior to his "official retirement."

Along the way, Steve also taught courses in Maintenance Management, Planning and Design and Natural Resource Management for eight years as an Adjunct Professor at Aurora University in Aurora, Illinois. Since 1999, Plumb has also served as an instructor for the National Playground Safety Institute. As a Regent on the National Recreation and Park Association Maintenance Management School Board of Regents, he has also developed monographs and made presentations on Planning and Organizing the Maintenance Program, Safety and Risk Management, Computer Applications and Play Area Safety and Maintenance.

Under Plumb's supervision, both the Elmhurst and the Glenview, Illinois Park Districts were extensively revised and upgraded. Major accomplishments included the development and implementation of computerized Maintenance Management Systems, management of operating and capital budgets in excess of $2 million, and development of grant applications that resulted in more than $2 million in acquisition and development funds. In addition, many special facilities were developed and renovated, including swimming pools, an indoor ice-skating rink, golf courses, a skate park, an environmental education center, a health and racquet center and numerous trails. Further, during his tenure in both places, each District received the prestigious National Gold Medal for Excellence in Park and Recreation Management.

Of course, for Steve and others, there will always be an abundance of parks at the federal, state and local levels of government throughout the United States to inspect, to make recommendations, to bring about improvements or to simply help update. Furthermore, his current work provides an even greater level of challenges than his previous employment because each park system has different priorities, available resources and personnel, policies and operating procedures, funding levels and problems. For their part, Chicago-based parks are near the top of the pyramid in the U.S. in terms of having the resources, personnel and money to accomplish their goals.

Steve's other part-time assignment continues to involve teaching for the National Playground Safety Institute all over the U.S. The beauty of this part of his current job relates to working "when" he wants to do so and meshing the two assignments into one challenging, independent contractor business, which is headquartered out of his home. Of course, his income base begins with his retirement income plus benefits from the Elmhurst, Illinois Park District. Fortunately, Steve still receives relatively inexpensive health care benefits from Elmhurst. Then he is able to add his additional, two streams of income together to come up with a great outcome for him and his new wife Mary.

It was an exciting step to take for this modern-day, mountain man to get married again in his late 50's. For Mary, although still working in Chicago half time, life has changed even more radically. She left her friends and support system in suburban Chicago, married for the first time at age 52, and moved to a remote area in the Colorado mountains, approximately 80 miles from Colorado Springs, the nearest major city. In fact, Steve and Mary's mailbox is a 5-mile roundtrip, with the nearest grocery store or restaurant being more than 20 miles away. For the two of them, the remoteness has more advantages than disadvantages, including non-stop peace and quiet, beautiful views, great weather, mountains, no traffic or crowds and a much slower pace. Still, Steve indicated that making lists for major stores in Colorado Springs, such as Home Depot and Sam's Club has become a necessity of life.

Plumb commented that almost every day is sunny in the mountains of Colorado, where he has an 80-mile view out of his front window. He contrasted the weather, where he lives now, with the two to three weeks of clouds in the winter or early spring he used to experience in Chicago. He likes to play bridge, although he doesn't play as often now because of where he lives. He still plays some golf and rides his motorcycle. Plus, he and his wife enjoy hiking and just plain walking. In fact, he told me that last week, they went to the Grand Canyon together on a trip. Steve also enjoys reading, which he finds time to do in his new home. Finally, he rounds out his long, "honey do" list with many pictures he needs to frame and put on the walls in his mountain retreat. Recently, he told me that he actually spent $300 just on the framing glass he will need to get this particular job done.

Steve's assessment is that his life today is great in his newly constructed home in the mountains of Colorado, with his newly married wife and working in two different parts of an industry he loves. "What's not to like," he told me. Indeed, Steve took some risks, when he retired early, moved to Colorado, hired a builder to construct his home in the mountains, got married for the first time in approximately seven years (for him) and also set out to establish an independent contractor business model as an industry consultant and teacher. But, each of these steps has worked out, partly because of his philosophy to "make a decision, then make it right."

Plumb's example demonstrates clearly that life continues to have its risks, but it also has its share of rewards for those, who are willing to go boldly where few other men and women have gone before them.

Helen Richardson

Writer/Editor, Moved to Colorado

One of the nagging questions in life for Helen Richardson is exploring not only what is possible, but also finding out what is the most desirable mix of choices. Living in Pagosa Springs in southwestern Colorado may not be everyone's concept of an ideal setting, but it gets Richardson's vote. Specifically, she took early retirement from a Cleveland-based media company to move there with her husband and jointly pursue their interests in nature photography and the outdoors.

While Richardson grew up on a small farm in southeastern Ohio, she always considered herself a city girl. With a brand new degree in Home Economics education from Ohio University, she migrated north to Cleveland where she taught briefly, met her husband and began a family. A few years later, her first career transformation took place. Their children had reached an age of budding independence and Richardson felt the urge to return to work, but not as a teacher. She worked in several clerical positions with a publishing company and was fortunate to have a mentor, who gave her writing assignments and encouragement. Her opportunity happened when she lost a job just when Penton Media's Transportation & Distribution magazine was looking for a new assistant editor.

Richardson marshaled her experience and nerve and applied to an editor who found Helen's curiosity appealing. The best was yet to come. She discovered that that editor was also a superb teacher and she eagerly learned from him. The learning paid off in ever increasing responsibility and trust. Over 11 years, Richardson was transformed from a raw recruit to an award-winning editor. In fact, she suggested the concept for a new publication for women in logistics. The publisher approved the idea and even gave her responsibility for creating it. She won a journalism award for the newsletter its first year.

Time for a change

As satisfying as this career success was, at age 55, Richardson found herself thinking more and more frequently of leaving the corporate environment and becoming a freelance writer. Even though she appreciated her work and her colleagues there, she longed to rid herself of office politics and the daily commute. She and her husband both wanted to live where they could indulge in nature photography, literally, in their backyard. They also began to envision a new, more relaxed lifestyle. Their children had flown the nest and were already located in different parts of the country, which left no strong family ties to Cleveland. While it would be difficult to leave friends, new horizons beckoned.

Increasingly drawn to the quiet of a beautiful countryside, they found love at first sight on a vacation in the mountains of Colorado. During repeated trips to Colorado and Utah, Helen Richardson and her husband began thinking seriously about relocating. They concluded he would retire and she would continue writing, but as a freelancer. From that point, the planning and decision-making process was much less scientific than a lot of others would consider necessary, but the end result was surprisingly positive.

The density of national parks in Colorado and Utah suggested the Richardsons could find happiness in the Four Corners area. For a number of reasons – taxes, climate, scenery, family – Colorado was the most appealing choice.

In the final analysis, Helen and her husband looked at several small towns but agreed Pagosa Springs had an edge because a close relative planned to retire there also. The small mountain town lacked a college for continuing education nor did it have a hospital, conditions both had agreed should be part of their retirement location package. But the population was small, the scenery inviting and it was definitely rural.

In house hunting, reality came to the forefront. Richardson dreamed of 35 acres far from anything. Her husband felt city water and sewer service were a must as well as being within the fire protection district. Practicality won, they purchased a small home with terrific mountain views on an acre of land on a dirt road near town and began a new phase of their lives with no regrets. The location was a happy choice for both as Richardson soon had companions for her morning walk. The fact that elk, deer, bear and bobcats frequent the yard left no need to be in a more remote location.

While Richardson continued to work as a freelance writer, her husband was officially retired. However, they both wanted to become active members of the community. A couple of opportunities surfaced rather quickly that helped them meet this goal.

With more than a passing interest in the ancient cultures of the Southwest, the Richardsons attended an open house at a local archaeological site. They both became active volunteers and discovered a new path for learning as well as a way to meet their new neighbors. At the same time, the couple was invited to attend a newcomers group function. The large crowd was a turnoff, but a spin-off activity was more to their liking. Taking turns hosting and attending small-group dinners allowed Helen and her husband to get to know other newcomers and make new friends.

Making it work

From her office overlooking the San Juan Mountains, Richardson writes for a variety of clients including Industry Week, Food Logistics, Supply Chain e-Business and World Trade. She has also edited books on the history of logistics, change management, courage in leadership and Vietnam. Today, her greatest challenge is balancing her quality of life. Does she take on another assignment at the risk of having to pass up the next wildflower hike? Yet, if she spends too much time playing, it's tough to meet the high cost of living her dream.

Cost of living is high in a remote small town, such as Pagosa Springs. Everything has to travel long distances to reach stores. Shoppers are a captive audience– the nearest Wal-Mart is an hour away, the closest mall of any size is two hours away in Farmington, New Mexico.

As a nearly 60 year old retiree, Helen has to pay her own health insurance costs. Fortunately, she remains healthy enough to make that affordable, but watches self-employed friends with health problems struggle to meet astronomical fees for private health insurance. The lack of a hospital turned out to be a non-issue. Health-care crises with family and friends resulted in exemplary care.

Living in a remote location is inconvenient when business travel is necessary because Pagosa Springs is an hour from the nearest commercial airport– one that accommodates only commuter jets. So any trip involves multiple legs or a drive to a bigger airport in Albuquerque, NM, nearly five hours away. Fortunately for Richardson, business travel is infrequent.

College classes are vaguely missed along with culture in general. Yet local theater productions provide amazing talent. Fort Lewis College, an hour away in Durango, provides a number of cultural opportunities. And an hour and a half away, Creede's Repertory Theater provides outstanding entertainment.

Small-town politics are often frustrating with too many would-be leaders and too strong of a good-ole-boy network. City planning keeps getting rehashed with no action taken to preserve the small-town environment and the beauty that attracts ever more people to the area.

The weather is a constant surprise. Winters are cold and the snow is, hopefully, deep, but the humidity stays low. Richardson didn't believe it could make so much difference, but regularly walks in sub-freezing temperatures. Even if the snowplow doesn't reach her street after a storm, SUVs pack the snow and make it passable. Working at home means she doesn't have to leave the house anyway. And the pine forest turns into a winter wonderland after each snowfall.

Summers feature hot dry days but blissfully cool nights. Winter and summer, there are far more days of sunshine than overcast. Gardening is a challenging hobby as Richardson learns more about xeriscaping and water conservation in her new high-desert environment.

Certainly, one aspect of pursuing our over-50 dreams must include the ability to work and live in the place of our dreams. Helen Richardson and her husband made that choice and so can each of us.

• Now What? •

Chapter Seven

• Now What? •

Donald J. Delandro

Retired BG, Started a Company

His general staff officer buddies couldn't believe it, but Donald J. Delandro had actually decided not to pursue a lucrative career as a future Pentagon contractor. Of course, what Brigadier General Donald Delandro was rejecting was the all too common revolving door, which former President Dwight D. Eisenhower had warned America about in a famous speech near the end of his second term of office.

Instead, at the end of his nearly 30-year career in the U. S. Army in 1985, Delandro chose to start a firm called Arrow Supply Company for an old army buddy. This company was the forerunner for Affordable Supply Company Inc. (ASCO), which was designed to give something back to the inner-city, black community of Washington, DC. ASCO, Delandro's current company start-up, has actually gone from $17,000 initially to approximately $2.3 million in annual sales today. Today, Delandro directs all activities of this minority-owned enterprise, which includes marketing, financial management, personnel administration, inventory management, government relationships, contractual negotiations and representation functions.

Initially, Donald J. Delandro was commissioned as a Second Lieutenant, Infantry in 1956. In 1958, he transferred to the Adjutant General's Corps. Ultimately, he attained the rank of Brigadier General in 1981. Over the years, this hard-charger held numerous positions, which culminated in his being named the Adjutant General of the Army (TAG). As TAG, Delandro directed the efforts of approximately 2,700 men and women worldwide in executing personnel and administrative functions within the U.S. Army.

Today, Delandro's experience in community relations has led him to become an active supporter of numerous organizations. He has even served as Chairman of the Board of Trustees for IDEA Public Charter High School and Chairman of the Advisory Board for Our Lady of Peace Catholic School. He is also a member of the Community Business Partnership of the Greater Washington Board of Trade and a member of the Retired Military Officers Association (RMOA).

For his part, Affordable Supply Company (ASCO) opened its doors during December, 1986. ASCO distributes janitorial, lighting, medical and disposable food service supplies. Delandro's company also operates warehouses, manages other facilities, and provides moving services, mail and distribution services plus courier and janitorial services.

In addition, ASCO now also provides administrative management support, computer operations, information technology and publications management. In the process, Affordable Supply Co. has emerged as a full-time service, supply and management company, with a wide ranging list of capabilities.

ASCO has also been HUBZONE certified by the Small Business Administration. Don has therefore expressed interest in a teaming arrangement with other companies, which desire a 10% preference in full and open competition. The District of Columbia has also certified ASCO as a small and disadvantaged business and recognized it as such for contracts in Washington, DC and in neighboring jurisdictions.

Beginning as a movement or idea in Metropolitan Washington, ASCO became a way to demonstrate that a start-up company could become successful in the inner city. Purposefully located in the Marshall Heights community of northeast Washington, DC, the company focuses on the recruitment, training and development of young, high school graduates. As an important note of explanation, this part of the District chronically suffers high unemployment among its youth. In fact, ASCO's growth in sales and employment has allowed it to have a growing impact within the minority community as it employs more young people and delivers more service. Its slogan of "Prompt Delivery of Quality Products and Services at Affordable Prices" not only says a lot about the company, but also about its owner Donald J. Delandro (BG Retired).

The hopeful part of Delandro's story is this: there are men and women, who choose to make career decisions, for reasons other than a large paycheck after a distinguished career in the military. In fact, there are men and women, who choose to give back to the community, which blessed them and gave them a wonderful opportunity in this great land, which is America.

Laurie Dellinger

Inside Sales Agent, Became Hair Stylist/Manicurist

J ust before her 50th birthday, Laurie Dellinger got laid off from her inside sales position at Guardian Electric in Woodstock, Illinois. After 10 years on the job, she had rated six weeks of severance. Several years before that, her 50 year old husband, who was involved with Ramp Services at Northwest Airlines Cargo, had been killed in a tragic automobile accident. Together, they had owned a 20 acre horse ranch in Union, Illinois, which her husband had wanted to work after his anticipated retirement at age 55.

But, things turned out differently than Laurie had expected. The love of her life died unexpectedly and she no longer wanted to own or run a horse ranch. That just wasn't her McHenry County, Illinois dream. In addition, both of her parents had died in fairly quick succession to one another three years after her husband died.

As a young woman, Dellinger had dropped out of college due to a lack of direction in her life. Then, she had joined United Airlines, when she met and married her husband Robert. As a high school grad, her husband had particularly liked his Northwest Airlines job, as a means of providing for his family. "Where else," he told Laurie, "could someone with a high school education make this much money working as a fork lift operator?" Of course, the benefits at Northwest were also great, Dellinger noted.

So, what was she to do now? And, where was the relatively young widow to go? Also, where could she turn for help? As she thought through her options, she took two months off, in essence to help clear the cobwebs from within her brain.

As she went through this process, Dellinger sought and received a limited amount of help from the State of Illinois as a displaced worker, which she didn't continue to receive for long. She also sold her horse ranch, paid off the mortgage and bought a condominium in Woodstock, Illinois for cash. With some money left over from the ranch proceeds and with some inheritance from both of her parents, Laurie was then able to establish a nest-egg, which everyone simply doesn't have. In addition, she had received life insurance proceeds plus a settlement from the company which employed the man, who had accidentally killed her husband in the automobile accident.

Now, she was ready to conquer the world. Her choice was to sign up for beauty school, which frequently is a choice men and women make in their 20s versus 50s. But, what an adventure it turned out to be. In addition, as an older student, Dellinger found herself much more motivated to learn and study. The next 18 months, which included an on-the-job training segment as well at Hair 2000 in Wauconda and Hair Directors in Woodstock, where she ultimately ended up, seemed to fly.

Now, she was able to do something that she really wanted to do and she could also talk all she wanted on her job. In her last assignment before beauty school, she had sometimes gotten in trouble for "visiting" too much on the job. But now, talking was actually a part of her "new" occupation's requirements.

Initially, her business started slowly, but then it continued to build as more and more women and men found out about Laurie Dellinger at the Hair Directors on the Square in Woodstock, Illinois. In fact, Dellinger commented that perhaps the owner of her shop actually hired her, in part, because she was older and because of the age and the amount of money many of her baby boomer friends and clients could spend on such items as a manicure or pedicure, in addition to the normal range of salon services.

Yes, it's scary to make a move, even when we have to do so. "What if I can't learn?" we frequently think to ourselves.

"After all, it has been 30 years since I was last in school," we say to ourselves as if to justify failure ahead of time.

But, the hopeful part of this story is that with some additional education in our lives, our options change and our income often goes up. Further, that's not just true for younger workers in our society, but for over the age of 50 employees and independent contractors, as well. In fact, it's not too late by any means to start being a beautician at age 52. Ask Laurie Dellinger if that didn't happen for her.

Chapter Eight

• Now What? •

Future Shock: Employment/Job Trends Look Promising!

Recently, this author caught up with Leigh Branham, his former roommate and friend from Journalism Graduate School at the University of Missouri-Columbia. Since their education together, Branham has enjoyed 30 years of experience in business, education and management consulting in his mission of helping employers implement best practices in employee engagement and retention.

In 2001, Leigh Branham authored "Keeping the People Who Keep You in Business: 24 Ways to Hang On to Your Most Valuable Talent" (AMACOM, 2001), which consistently ranks on Amazon.com as one of the best-selling books on employee retention. His newest book is "The 7 Hidden Reasons Employees Leave: How to Recognize the Subtle Signs and Act Before It's Too Late."

Leigh was Vice President, Organizational Consulting with Right Management Consultants in Kansas City and Leader of the firm's Talent Management Practice in the Heartland Region. Prior to that, he was Senior Consultant with Lee Hecht Harrison in Irvine, California.

He has been widely quoted in the media, including *Fortune*, *BusinessWeek* and The Associated Press, as an expert on employee retention. He also writes a regular commentary on managing talent for *The Kansas City Star*.

Branham holds Masters degrees in Counseling/Personnel Services and Journalism from the University of Missouri – Columbia and a Bachelor's degree in English Literature from Vanderbilt University. Leigh is a member of the Society of Human Resource Management and The Organizational Development Network. He can be contacted at LB@keepingthepeople.com.

The following Question and Answer exchange is introduced to the readers of this book, as a bird's eye view from an HR expert, who anticipates the upcoming labor market perhaps more clearly than most of us see it in the United States. Of course, when these developments begin to take place, they will become clear for everyone to understand. But, today, beyond the politics of the immediate job concerns and pressures, a far different labor market is only now beginning to emerge.

Question: What is your general observation about the US job market over the next 5 years for men and women, who are at least 50 years old today?

Answer: The US job market has never been as hard to predict as it is today, due to the extreme economic and political volatility that has existed since 9/11. We are indeed in uncharted waters. Although we cannot forecast when and of what magnitude the next terrorist act may occur, and what impact it will have on the world's economies, there are some things that are within the realm of predictability. Of these, the foremost is the demographic fact that there are approximately 78 million baby boomers born between 1946 and 1963, but only 45 million Generation Xers, who were born between 1964 and 1980. Those in the leading edge of the baby boom have now just turned 60. Some have retired already, but many are contemplating retirement at 62, though most will retire when full social security benefits kick in, at 66 (beginning in 2012). Those now turning 50 were born in 1956, so each year for the next six years a new class of boomers will turn 50. Then, in 2012, the first "class" of leading edge boomers will begin to retire in big numbers.

What this means for boomers is that as time passes and more of them "retire" or accelerate a gradual, albeit not total withdrawal from the workforce, they will be in greater demand. Why? Simple – there are not enough Xers in the workforce to take their places, especially in filling more senior management positions that will become vacant.

Q: *How do you see that analysis changing for the 5 years after that for these same men and women versus the first five year trend line?*

A: During the second five years – 2011-2016 – the labor shortage will worsen year by year at least through 2020, when Generation X workers will begin to move into the management ranks in big numbers, thus taking up the slack. So, opportunities for boomers who want to keep working will be there in big numbers and in many forms (part-time, temp, consulting, entrepreneurial, volunteering, public service, work-from-home and job sharing) for years to come.

Of course, there are many other trends that must be accounted for and grow harder to predict the farther out one looks into the future. Among them are many that will serve to mitigate the labor shortage:

- increased outsourcing and off-shoring;
- job elimination due to computer automation and the growth of customer self-service;
- Increasing US trade deficits;
- many baby boomers opting to stay in the job market for financial and non-financial reasons;
- the influx of foreign workers and immigrants;
- an economy that is no longer growing and creating jobs as it was in the 1980's or 1990's; and
- the increasing productivity that businesses have learned to sustain by doing more with fewer workers.

Q: *What industries or occupation categories will see labor shortages first, as baby boomers begin to retire?*

A: Healthcare will be the most dramatic, especially in nursing, but in all job categories as the demand for health care services for aging boomers grows. Others include IT workers, computer technicians, entry-level service staff in restaurants, hotels and retail stores, pharmacists, assisted living employees, financial service workers and construction workers, to name a few where shortages already exist.

Q: *Will part-time working options be pursued by our baby boom generation, as we transition from full-time jobs?*

A: Absolutely. Many boomers have been pushing themselves hard for years. Some say that the current generation of boomers may be the most burned-out and stressed out generation of workers ever. So many are looking to downshift by going part-time, and if they choose to work part-time, many will make sure it is doing something less stressful and more intrinsically enjoyable than what they were doing full-time during their peak earning years.

Q: *Will Generation Xers be able to fill in the blanks in this labor market equation?*

A: No, they will not, because there are simply not enough of them. The good news for Xers is that they will be in high demand and will be courted by employers, especially those in high-demand occupations. Many will move into management positions sooner than they otherwise would have, although millions of Xers want no part of corporate life. Those who do will work fewer hours and have more work-life balance than boomers ever did. And a much higher percentage of Xers will pursue entrepreneurial options than boomers did.

Q: What other factors will be relevant for baby boomers, as they phase out of full-time jobs?

A: They will define retirement differently than their parents did. Instead of defining retirement as moving to Florida or Arizona and playing golf full-time, many will want to combat loneliness by maintaining a community of working relationships. Others will continue to seek meaning and self-fulfillment – hallmark values of the boomer generation – by seeking work that is more inherently enjoyable. Some will pursue public service or volunteer work. Increasingly, retirement may not be defined as working fewer hours, but as spending a higher proportion of hours worked doing the things we most enjoy doing. That is, in fact, how I will continue to define retirement for myself because from a strictly financial standpoint, I don't ever see full-time retirement as a realistic option. I also hope to have some discretionary talent to develop hidden or unused skills/vocations that I never had time to pursue earlier – such as drawing, painting and fiction writing.

Q: *Will baby boomers increasingly work longer, until age 70 for example?*

A: Yes, I think many more individuals will do that than in previous generations. Some will do so because they have to work, but others will make that choice because they will be in better health than those at the same age in previous generations and will be able to do so at increasingly advanced ages. It will not be uncommon for boomers to work into their 80s as long as they are healthy.

Q: *What part will good health play in the overall equation for the baby boomers?*

A: Of course, most boomers are healthier than previous generations and will be beneficiaries of better medicines, new procedures and other bio-technological advances. Many have also grown increasingly interested as they have aged in fitness and preventive health measures.

Q: *What part will travel and other leisure pursuits play for baby boomers, as they enter into this over age 50 time of their lives?*

A: Boomers stand to inherit more wealth than any generation ever, so they will have the wherewithal to travel and pursue many leisure interests, many of which require more activity and fitness. The market for adventure vacations has already increased among boomer travelers.

Q: What part will outsourcing play in the trend lines for over 50 year olds in the future?

A: This one is hard to predict because of the instability of the world economy, but it appears that the outsourcing trend will continue for the immediate future.

Q: What role will continuing education play in this mix of factors for over 50 year olds?

A: Continuing education will be an outlet for the boomer's drive for learning and self-fulfillment. For many, it will take the form of learning new hobbies, while others will increase their reading. Still others will seek new avenues for learning by computer. Also, many boomers will return to community colleges, both as students and as teachers.

Q: What part will someone's willingness to move to another part of the US play in our future economy?

A: Every generation seems to be more mobile than the last, and this should be no exception with boomers. Most of the economic growth appears to be happening in Sun Belt states such as Florida, Texas, Arizona and California, which would reinforce historic patterns of migration for retirees. However, because of the anticipated labor shortages, many retirees will find work and housing options in non-traditional retirement locations, as well. Some will even retire to Mexico, where many are just now beginning to discover incredible bargains in real estate.

As has always been the case, one's willingness to move will continue to make more work options available for the individual and will help fill many of the jobs that might otherwise have gone unfilled.

Q: Will companies themselves need to do more in order to keep and promote their best employees?

A: This is the central message of the two books I have written – "Keeping the People Who Keep You in Business" (2001) and "The 7 Hidden Reasons Employees Leave" (2005). As the "war for talent" returns, employers will have to compete for talent to achieve their business objectives, much as they were forced to do in the late 90's. More companies will seek to be known as "great places to work," and will implement more employee-centered benefits and enlightened management practices.

Employers' attitudes toward older and retiring workers will also have to change. Companies will make unprecedented efforts to keep retiring workers on a part-time basis or as mentors to younger workers and as full-time project leaders.

We are also likely to see much less discrimination in the hiring of older workers as the labor shortage continues to worsen over the next 15 years.

Q: What other factors should men and women, who are currently over age 50, know about to a greater degree than they currently realize?

A: Many are woefully ignorant of financial planning and a remarkable number have not even started planning for their retirement. Given the current unpredictability regarding social security benefits, this is alarming. This is why financial planning is a growth industry and will continue to be for years to come.

Chapter Nine

• Now What? •

Bill Beyer

FAA Staffer, Became a Home
Remodeler/Landlord

A recently retired support staff member from the Federal Aviation Agency (FAA) Kansas City Region, where he had earlier served as an air traffic controller, Bill Beyer today remodels homes and duplexes and then rents them out to lower income families, who don't often encounter such well maintained housing choices. His clients often turn out to lower-income women with children in the Kansas City area.

In the process, Beyer has developed and continues to expand his real estate portfolio as a long-term investment tool. So, how did Bill at age 52 arrive at this career decision? Here's the story.

Earlier, this Independence, Missouri-based small business executive had actually built his own home 17 years ago for his wife Kyle (which is actually her middle name, which she likes to use) and their two children. In fact, Bill's daughter Emily married my son Jim Armstrong two years ago and they, too, live in the Greater Kansas City area. Jim recently commented to me that Bill is quite "a handy guy," based on having worked with his father-in-law, who has helped the young couple paint rooms and wallpaper, for example, in their recently purchased first home. As a not uninterested outside observer, the term unselfish would also seem to fit Bill Beyer quite nicely.

For his part, Beyer graduated from Central Missouri State University in Warrensburg, Missouri, which is located about 50 miles from Kansas City, with a degree in teaching. After that, he taught high school math, while serving as both a football coach and a wrestling coach for seven years. But, his father kept urging his son to at least take the examination to become an air traffic controller. At the time, a younger Bill just didn't think that's what he wanted to do. However, to get his Dad to quit asking him to do so, he took the test. But, at the time, there was no shortage of air traffic controllers in the U.S. At least that statement was true before the now famous 1981 Air Traffic Controllers Strike, which was settled by our commander-in-chief, Ronald Reagan, firing the striking air traffic controllers.

That's when the call came from the FAA for Bill Beyer to start training in Oklahoma City the next week. Well, three weeks later, he actually did report to Oklahoma City and thus began his career as an air traffic controller for the next 20 years. Then, Bill served as a support staffer for the next 1 1/2 years. At that point, he was faced with a rather interesting decision that went something like this. He could take an early retirement option, which would give him 50% of his former pay by simply being at least 50 years old and having 20 years of service. But, he had to retire no later than the mandatory age of 56. However, in both cases, the pay formula in this particular case would be the same. Now, the math doesn't always work that way, but in Bill's case that's how it turned out.

So, the operative question became what to do after that point for Bill Beyer? He briefly considered going back to teaching, but then decided against that option. Several years earlier, he had also considered the possibility of going into full-time ministry. In fact, in this instance, he had actually gone so far as to take and complete 20 hours of graduate work toward a Masters of Divinity degree through a local Christian seminary. But, he decided that this direction, too, was ultimately not what he wanted to do. He had also thought briefly about building houses from scratch, which he had done on one other occasion beyond his own home. That venture had turned out positively, but Bill knew going forward that it would hold considerable risks as a full-time endeavor.

Then, one of Bill's friends, who was quite a successful realtor, met with Beyer and presented another very intriguing option. Why not simply remodel an existing home, he asked, instead of beginning from scratch? Then, he explained, Bill could either sell or rent these Section 8 homes, which also qualify for government assistance, and other types of housing units to people, who were badly in need of such housing. The friend further explained that if Beyer didn't sell a given home, he would also be building a future real estate investment portfolio.

After thinking about and also praying about this option, Bill Beyer chose to pursue the home remodeler/landlord route for several reasons. First, he felt that he could really make a difference for women who were not used to having someone even try to make a real effort in their lives. Second, Beyer was also a conservative investor and this approach appealed to this side of his nature, too. Further, he was still able to receive lower cost medical insurance and other benefits from the FAA through a generous, early retirement package.

So, Bill Beyer took the plunge at age 51, in part, due to his strong interest in working with his hands and especially because it involved remodeling versus home building. Of course, once he completes the rehabs, then Beyer has also found it's easier to find renters than buyers. In the meantime, the equity position continues to increase every month, as his tenants basically pay his payments, he commented.

With a current and future housing shortage projected for the foreseeable future, Bill Beyer has succeeded and will in the future because he builds clean, safe and attractive homes for lower-income women and their children, who can really use a break. Plus, his profession and the way he practices it really takes on a dimension of ministry in the marketplace for Bill and, in the process, gives him great satisfaction.

Long active in his suburban Baptist church in the Kansas City area with his wife Kyle, Beyer represents the kind of good neighbor we should all strive to be.

• Now What? •

Alfreda Bruen

Pharmacist, Filled Healthcare Need

Welcome to Fairfield Bay, which is an active adult community just north of Little Rock, Arkansas and is also the home base today for pharmacist, Alfreda Bruen.

The good news about Alfreda's story overall has to do with the nationwide shortage of pharmacists. Yes, there are many offers for men and women everywhere, who are qualified pharmacists, including someone who is today age 70. Specifically, Bruen works part-time at two different hospitals during the month and also one day each week at a retail pharmacy near her home in Fairfield Bay.

The first of these assignments involves working one day each month at Conway Regional Hospital essentially just to stay current. The second assignment in Heber Springs, Arkansas, which is an affiliate of the well known Baptist Hospital in Little Rock, involves working two to three days each month as the only pharmacist on duty that day in the

111

rural setting of Heber Springs, Arkansas in their 15 bed hospital.

In this instance, Alfreda helps the normal pharmacist take a day off by simply working for him or her. The final assignment involves Bruen working one day each week at a retail pharmacy near her home.

But, the good news about an independent contractor status for this pharmacist, who works for three different employers each month, is that it allows Bruen to travel, when she wants to do so, because she sets her own schedule based upon other demand factors beyond simply work.

Alfreda Bruen began her career after graduating from the Temple University School of Pharmacy in Philadelphia, Pennsylvania, with a Bachelor of Science degree in 1955. Prior to her family's move to Arkansas, she most recently worked at St. Francis Hospital in Memphis, where she served as the Schedules Supervisor in a 700 bed hospital in order to provide 24 hour staffing with 21 pharmacists on staff. Also before the move, Bruen functioned in a consultant role for St. Francis Nursing Home, which was a 100 bed acute care nursing facility. In this capacity, Alfreda was responsible for monthly chart reviews as required by HCVA, supplying the medications, billing and providing instruction on medications to the nursing staff.

Alfreda also actively volunteers her time on a generous basis. For example, this other-focused star currently serves on the board of directors for Boston Mountain Rural Clinic, which covers five locations that serve four counties near her home. Alfreda also sings in her church choir at the local Methodist church and she serves there on a committee, which is called the Care & Nurture Committee. Specifically, she helps to drive men and women, particularly other seniors from her area, to the doctor or for a chemotherapy session, for example. In other instances, if someone has lost a spouse and can no longer drive himself/herself, that individual may simply have a basic transportation need, which Alfreda and other committee members help to address. Her church committee also delivers meals on wheels to other senior men and women every day.

Fun and recreation also help round out the picture for this great-grandmother. Her family includes her husband George, who is a retired naval aviator and whose second profession was a high school naval science instructor, three children, seven grandchildren and two great grandchildren. Two of her three children live with their families, which includes five grandchildren, in Memphis, while one of her three children lives in Houston with a family that includes two children there.

Alfreda Bruen, who is a young, great grandmother, has lived for the last 10 years in Arkansas. She enjoys activities ranging from golf, perhaps one day each week, to tennis to yard work. In warmer weather, she and her husband George enjoy going out on the lake in their pontoon boat. Alfreda also very much enjoys attending meetings once each month with the Red Hat Society, which is a group of active, older women who wear purple and red hats. They go out together and simply enjoy fun activities like bowling, lunch or dinner. Plus, three to four times each week, Bruen works out at a local fitness center for an hour each time, where she even lifts weights. Because Alfreda doesn't want her overall body strength and health to degenerate, she stays active and fit by choosing those workout activities, which keep her muscles in top shape.

Alfreda Bruen has likewise joined the American Society for Consultant Pharmacists and last year attended the organization's annual meeting in San Antonio in order to complete her yearly credit requirements for license renewal.

The hopeful part of this story focuses less on where Alfreda lives and more on her unique skill set, which continues to be very much in demand nationwide. However, over and beyond work related issues, Alfreda has chosen to stay active and fit, as she enjoys herself, her husband, her children, grandchildren and great grandchildren and as she lives life to the fullest in every possible way. And, for Alfreda, that also means giving of herself to serve the needs of her community and of her area. As Americans, we cannot help but salute those men and women, who choose to make that "extra" effort for the good of us all. Thank you and God bless you Alfreda Bruen.

Chapter Ten

• Now What? •

Jim McElyea

Corporate Attorney, Moved to Michigan

F irst, one friend saw the Time Magazine story about Jim McElyea's job search process and, then, another read it too. Soon, many people who knew Jim were commenting about the age bias piece from this important US magazine. The ironic twist in McElyea's case related to Jim's former job as Chief Legal Officer of a major Chicago company.

Most of us realize that such a development in our careers can happen to us. But, how could it take place with a former corporate legal counsel?

In the meantime, there was the support group from a local church, which ministered to men and women between jobs/careers, together with encouraging words from a handful of faithful friends. But, none of it really seemed to help this 48-year-old man. Lawyer Jim McElyea had actually advised executives at his former company on how to act and

117

what to say, when a prospect was interviewing for a job. But, now, he was the one interviewing himself.

An interim solution emerged for Jim to work on a part-time basis as a general practitioner in the legal profession. Of course, the income spread was enormous in comparison with his former assignment. But, McElyea put his head down and continued to interview for other corporate assignments.

Specifically, after 20 months in pursuit of a different outcome, Jim McElyea once again got the nod to serve as Chief Legal Officer for still another Chicago-based company. The hopeful outcome for this man and all of us over age 50 only came through hard work and perseverance, while choosing not to give up in the process.

And, so, the word of hope for any of us, who find ourselves in a similar position today, is simply to PERSEVERE.

In the process, this divorced father of one son had also begun to date a never-before-married, 45-year-old woman from his church. Madge or Maggie, as Jim called her, had served as the Administrator of First Presbyterian Church of River Forest, Illinois. She had dated to some degree over the years, but nothing had really developed into a marriage for her. At a strategic point in their relationship, Jim McElyea proposed to Maggie, the two of them got married and together began to raise his son, Patrick, whose mother had died tragically.

And, so, their lives changed not only in terms of each of their respective jobs, but also in terms of every other aspect of their personal circumstances, too. Those changes were hard, while also rewarding at the same time.

In the meantime, several different corporate owners came and went at the packaging company for Chief Legal Officer Jim McElyea, while his family continued to live and thrive in the Chicagoland area. Then, something truly wonderful, while at the same time surprising to most of us as outside observers, took place in Jim's life and the life of his family. Specifically, the "new" parent company of his Chicago-based subsidiary offered Jim a promotion to the corporate headquarters in the same capacity, with even more responsibility and a higher income.

In fact, the McElyea family now got to move to Ann Arbor, Michigan so that Jim could work for the $5 billion parent corporation. Plus, their "new" home was located adjacent to a prestigious golf course development there, with their home right on the 3rd tee. For Jim's wife Maggie, this was actually the first time she had lived outside of Chicago in nearly 30 years. But, the whole process was a "new" adventure for the family and a real challenge in the new assignment for Jim McElyea.

So, what should we learn from this presentation in relationship to our own life circumstances? Simple. Even when a concern about possible age bias in our job search makes Time Magazine, that part of our lives doesn't have to be the end of the story. In fact, a great story in our lives can take place, which can even include a wonderful, "new" wife, custody of our children as a father and even the job of our dreams at a billion dollar plus corporation. Ask Jim McElyea if you don't believe it.

Sheri Tingey

Alaska Entrepreneur, Runs Alpacka Raft

Today, Sheri Tingey, who is age 60, runs a family business called Alpacka Raft, which has created and built a series of ultra light, packable rafts for use in long distance backpacking and wilderness racing.

Sometimes, a "new" business opportunity can begin with a challenge or a question from a friend or a loved one. And that's exactly what happened when Sheri's son, Thor, asked his mom to come up with a light-weight raft that could stand up to some of the most demanding parts of Alaska's wilderness in a sport, where he was an enthusiast.

In the first year Sheri Tingey's Alpacka Raft sold 200 carefully crafted units, but had demand beginning to pick up outside of her Alaska base. In other words, if the rafts were strong enough to withstand Alaska's wilderness, the challenges from the Lower 48 would be easily surmountable, many potential buyers must have thought. In the process, sales have inched up from 200 to 400 and this year Tingey estimates that her sales will top 700 units from her whole product line with approximately $500 thousand in sales.

So, how did she wind up in Alaska so far away from her Arizona roots? After graduation from the University of Oregon with a degree in Physical Education, Sheri headed to Jackson Hole, Wyoming to ski for just "one season" before getting on with the real world. But, while she was there, she fell in love with skiing and tried to figure out a way to make a living besides waitressing. That is how she happened to start her first business, which involved making custom ski wear. Her one-piece snow gear for skiers at the time was sold through six retail shops around the U.S. including Sun Valley, Idaho, Aspen and Vail, Colorado, Alta and Snowbird, Utah, Jackson Hole, Wyoming and Lake Placid, New York. In that chapter of her life, Sheri would ski all day and, then, she sewed late in the evening every night.

After selling her "Design by Sheri" business, which she ran from 1967 to 1982 and which was based in Jackson Hole, Wyoming, she and her husband together with their two children moved to Alaska primarily because of a job offer for her husband. But, Sheri had also wanted to sell her business, in part, due to a series of health-related challenges she was experiencing, including chronic fatigue syndrome.

After moving to Alaska, Tingey again tried to sew, but the effort simply drained her. She desperately wanted her old energy level back and, as a consequence, felt rotten because it just wasn't coming back. At the time, her children were small and there were no programs available for them in the Alaska Bush. So, she wound up starting both a swimming and a gymnastics program for rural Alaska kids. Further, since Sheri was able to control the hours, she could also closely monitor how much energy she put out. Doing those morning or afternoon only programs, she could work these job assignments into the three good hours she had each day, where she functioned somewhat normally.

Today, Sheri has been married to her husband Ralph Tingey for 30 years. But, Sheri's inspiration for her current business, which came at the point in life where she was just beginning to feel good again after a nearly 20 year battle back to health, was and is her son Thor. For his part, Thor Tingey recently took several steps back from the business in order to attend law school. So, Tingey has recently taken a partner, Jim Jager, into the business to help her accomplish some of the things Thor or her husband had previously done in the business up to the time that a suitable business partner could be found. Finally, Sheri's daughter Daphne, who is 23, will be resuming school this fall near Boulder, Colorado, where she will continue her junior year at Naropa University in Psychology.

For Sheri Tingey and her husband, they had always wanted to move to Alaska, which she described as a state that someone either really loves or leaves it. From the beginning, she said, she and her family always kept a large dog team for racing in Alaska, even when her kids were little. Plus, she said that despite her chronic fatigue, running her dogs was not as tiring as someone might think and she very much enjoyed the experience. She really loves the wilderness in Alaska, she said, because it offers wonderful freedom to its residents. In addition, Sheri also loves to fish, hike, climb and do any kind of boating. Plus, she loves animals. And, Sheri still loves to sew and to build (which for her means carpentry work). In fact, Tingey describes the similarities between sewing and carpentry and said it was unfortunate that more people, both men and women, don't enjoy the cross-over benefits of both disciplines. Finally, Sheri loves to read too.

In terms of her health struggles, changing her MD to someone else who was willing to try some alternative approaches to medicine, made all the difference in regaining her health. Not just vitamins, but Sheri was willing to experiment with a wider range of treatment options than most physicians are willing to utilize. In the end, this alternative medicine approach essentially worked for her. Interestingly, Sheri's health had substantially improved just at the point of her son's challenge.

In turn, Mom Tingey was then excited and challenged to return to the passion of her life, which has long been design. As a child, her grandmother had taught her to sew. But, she came by the design part of her DNA make up quite naturally.

In the future, Sheri concluded that she and her husband may decide to take off from November through the end of

January, when Alaska experiences that long night in the state. Like many other Alaskans their age, they would then plan to come back by February 1st each year.

Her greatest business challenge comes down to correctly estimating the demand for her product ahead of time each year and, then, having it manufactured by Feathercraft Kayaks, which uses this down time to produce her rafts. For its part, Feathercraft Kayaks has long been known for making amazing folding kayaks. In addition, Tingey has recently overcome still another nagging problem by no longer sub-contracting to her brother-in-law in Phoenix to glue the bottoms into her rafts. Because he had previously used a bothersome glue, she changed back to Feathercraft to finish the raft they had started. Plus, the Feathercraft answer now includes a 100% environmentally friendly solution to gluing the bottom of the raft to complete the finished product. In fact, coming up with an environmentally acceptable glue has long been a challenge for all of the raft manufacturers, she confided.

Today, Sheri Tingey takes pride in her workmanship at Alpacka Raft. Now that she has been given a second chance in life to be a designer, she simply wants to make each raft last. Her short-hand way of putting it is this: "I'm just too old to make junk." From being a classic, drop-through-the-cracks kid, Sheri has found her niche, where she excels. Plus, she makes a quality product that anyone would be proud to call their own. Since her rafts can easily last for 15 to 20 years, each year, she has to find a whole series of new customers. But, each new raft she plans and makes is built to last. And, that's why Sheri Tingey easily qualifies as our "Alaska Entrepreneur Extraordinaire."

Chapter Eleven

• Now What? •

John Wehling

Retired St. Louis Teacher, Turned Gentleman Farmer

What can someone say about a friend you've known since kindergarten at Avery School in Webster Groves, Missouri? John Wehling, who was a playmate of mine when he and I were both five years old, today lives the life of a gentleman farmer who is pursuing his hobby interest in Beaufort, Missouri.

Wehling retired about two years ago after teaching math at Lindbergh High School in St. Louis County, Missouri for 33 years. For many years he taught the smartest high school students who had qualified for advanced or honors math classes, as well as those students who either couldn't or just didn't get it. Now, under the Missouri Teacher's Retirement System, he actually qualified at the relatively young age of 55 to retire with nearly 88% of his former salary (plus annual increases mandated under the plan).

Because John was smart and because he also understood the way the system was set up, he just never stopped going to college and graduate school, he said, until he had completed his MS ED in 1972 from Southern Illinois University Edwardsville. Then, he continued his education and, in the process, completed an additional 30 hours of graduate school in Mathematics, as well. These combined steps together put him into the best pay grade possible for a high school teacher and, over time, made his profession really pay off for him in terms of its max potential pay scale. Ultimately, all of these efforts also paid off in terms of his retirement pay and other benefits as well.

In John Wehling's life, his first wife Kay died unexpectedly from breast cancer in her 20s, while his second marriage ended with two sons and a divorce. But, his third walk down the aisle with a fellow teacher has proven to be a successful choice for him and for his wife Beth, who had never before been married.

Beth Wehling, who is a former 7th grade social studies Teacher of the Year in the State of Missouri, still works in school since she is younger than John and also because she just loves what she does.

Living with his wife Beth in Des Peres, Missouri after both of his grandparents had died on the farm, the question within the larger Wehling family became "What should our family do about the farm?" And, if we decide to keep it, "Who will look after it and take care of it?"

These questions in the last several years since John's retirement from teaching actually became even easier to figure out because he was the only one in the larger Wehling family who lived close enough to the farm to make a difference and who wasn't already working full-time. So, the process of elimination included the conclusion that no one in the family really wanted to sell his grandparents' farm. But, no one else had the time or the inclination to work it or look after it. Sometimes, choices merely present themselves to us for our final approval. In this case, this particular door opened for John and he is glad he chose to go through it.

Today, John drives his Mom, Sally, who is age 82, out to the farm, when she wants to go out there for a few days. He tinkers with an old tractor. He also supervises a "real farmer," who leases the farm's 220 acres to raise his crops of corn, soy beans and milo. And, he fixes things up around the place, which he really enjoys doing. Recently, he purchased another old tractor, a 1949 Farmall and restored it to useful condition.

Plus, he and his wife frequently just like to get away there for the weekend to clear out the cobwebs from their everyday cares of suburban St. Louis living.

For his part, John Wehling considers himself just an ordinary guy. And, yet, for the past 21 years, John has also pursued a disciplined diet and exercise regime that many of us would applaud, but few of us would actually follow. When it comes to working out, his stated philosophy is "I don't do much, but I do it."

Of course, an important part of reinventing ourselves also needs to focus on remaining or getting healthy through good choices, which need to include both eating right and exercise, according to all of the fitness experts and our own doctors.

Specifically, John works out five days each week for 45 minutes each time by alternating days of light calisthenics with days of walking. He also uses a tread mill and stationary bike to warm up and then he striates before each work out. In addition, in part because he knew that high blood pressure ran in his family, John has further made appropriate diet choices, which are both low in fat and low in salt. And, Wehling didn't just make this choice recently either. He actually came to this conclusion 21 years ago after his father's quadruple bypass surgery.

In addition, because John finally has the time, he now practices on his guitar and mandolin every day for three or more hours. Before, when he was still teaching, he would just be too tired at night to really make a serious effort on his music. But, now, he plays folk music and specializes in "old time." He also enjoys taking lessons once a week from a fabulous player and because of all the practice, Wehling has emerged as a much improved musician, he said. And, while he does play an occasional "paid gig," John admitted that he doesn't usually make that much money.

Wehling also believes in pursuing a continual, personal and spiritual search, where there are many paths to God. For his part, he believes that each person must discover his own path. He works on this area of his life every day, he said.

So, John Wehling really emerges as an excellent example of sticking with his plan by getting the best possible education he could or needed to get at the time, both for his immediate income then, plus his retirement pay now. Wehling also deserves a tip of our hats on the twin issues of diet and exercise. In other words, what he actually does today, we should also do.

In the process, an ordinary guy, who taught high school students for all of those years, has also now emerged as a gentleman farmer.

• Now What? •

Avis Marie Russell

Attorney at law, Moved to DC

In many ways, Avis Marie Russell grew up to become the daughter that any dad or mom would be proud to call his or her own. She earned her J.D. in May, 1979 from the Tulane University School of Law, where she was awarded the Hale Boggs Scholarship. At Tulane, Avis also served as the president of the Black Law Students Association. Russell had earlier graduated from Wellesley College in Wellesley, Massachusetts, where she earned her A.B. in Political Science in 1976.

Before his daughter went to Wellesley, her father Eugene Russell once told me that he had never even heard of Wellesley College. But, somehow, he and his family found a way to send her to this prestigious, Seven Sister School. What an opportunity Avis Russell received educationally! But, in the process, she also made the most of every open door on her way up the ladder to accomplishment and recognition.

Importantly, Russell also knew that both of her parents loved her and cared deeply about her. Her strength today, she believes, came especially from her mother Gloria, with whom she had always had a close and open relationship. For example, she said she could tell her mother anything, without fear of retribution or "getting into trouble."

Avis Russell, early in her career, was a commissioner and judge Ad Hoc in the Civil District Court for Orleans Parish (which is similar to a county jurisdiction) in Louisiana. In this role, she heard non-jury cases involving complex litigation and multi-party litigation referred by the district court judges for almost six years. Then, she would prepare written reasons, including finding of facts, conclusions of law and recommended judgments. Next, she spent nearly four years at a New Orleans law firm, where she was a partner at Simon, Peragine, Smith & Redfearn in New Orleans. There, she was involved in civil, litigation in state and federal trial and appellate courts, including construction, contracts, environmental law, insurance defense and product liability.

In her next assignment, Avis served for five plus years as City Attorney in the City of New Orleans, Department of Law. In this capacity, Russell provided legal advice to the Mayor, City Council and various departments of the New Orleans city government. She also managed a staff of 50 in-house attorneys and outside counsel in civil litigation, while also supervising attorneys, who prosecuted matters in municipal and traffic courts. In the process, Russell managed a $6 million department budget.

Her next appointment involved serving as Executive Counsel to the Mayor for nearly three years. In this capacity, she negotiated agreements for major economic development projects and union agreements. She also provided oversight for the procurement process in the management and operation of the Sewage and Water Board for the City of New Orleans, Louisiana.

Today, after taking nearly two years off to spend more time at home with her teenage and preteen daughters, while they were both still "in the house," Avis Marie Russell returned to work in her family's "new" hometown in Greater Washington, DC. In this instance, she has now served as General Counsel in the District of Columbia Water and Sewage Authority for the past two years. There she provides legal advice to the General Manager, Board of Directors and to the department directors, while also managing a legal staff and outside counsel.

Plus, along the way, Avis Russell has also been generous with her time by consistently giving back to the community in a long list of outside activities, especially during her time in the New Orleans area. In the process, she has also received an American Council of Career Women Achievers Award in 1991, the YWCA's New Orleans Role Model Award in 1992 and the Louisiana State Bar Association

Stephen Victory Award (for Outstanding Bar Journal article) in 1993.

Professionally, Avis Russell was asked to serve on the Louisiana Supreme Court Task Force on Racial and Ethnic Fairness in the Courts during 1993 and served on the National Bar Association Executive Committee from 1992 to 1994 and as Chair for the Partners in Majority Firms Division from 1993-1994, among other distinctions.

What does all of this past list of activities and accomplishments mean to Avis Marie Russell today? Well, first, she wanted most to help everyone in her family, certainly including her husband Robert, adjust to their move from New Orleans three years ago to the DC area due to a career move for her husband, where he is a partner in a prominent DC law firm where he specializes in labor and sports law. Russell also simply wanted "to be there" for her girls during at least some of their teenage years. Avis commented that she also really likes her work and her boss, who is both respectful of women and their abilities, she said. Russell also concluded that her current job duties and responsibilities don't involve the long hours now that she once worked in New Orleans nor is she involved in the same type of time-consuming political duties, which were once expected of her either.

Today, in her current job, she is involved with establishing legal procedures in her department and discussing how to automate a centralized filing system so that everyone can have immediate access to more detailed information about cases, for example.

She also commented that her time at home gave her a real sense of understanding about stay-at-home moms that she had never previously had. She also began to understand why so many of these women tend to defer to their husbands in matters of family finances, which she had never previously done. From their Bethesda, Maryland home, Avis and her family also had to search for a "new" church home for the first time in her whole life since she had always previously lived in New Orleans and had been a member of her parents' church for her whole life until the move to the DC area. Today, she and her family have joined a church close to their home, which is a multi-ethnic Methodist Church, with a focus on children. Avis serves as a member of the Board of Trustees. Her youngest daughter Rachel, who serves as an acolyte, will be confirmed at their new church.

In conclusion, Avis Marie Russell, who has excelled in a variety of legal assignments both in New Orleans and in Washington, DC, has long been an acknowledged leader and a role model in her community. Just before her mother Gloria died, she even told her daughter, "you will be fine without me." For her part, the life of Avis Russell certainly represents the conclusion to the ageless statement that "everything in life counts."

• Now What? •

Chapter Twelve

• Now What? •

James Armstrong

Missionary, Became a Pastor Again

A t 63, my Dad, Pastor Jim Armstrong, felt a strong calling to leave the day-to-day church ministry, which had been his life for almost 20 years, to go on short-term missionary/evangelism trips around the world. How did he even realize that such an option was possible?

Simple. A group of older minister friends, who were then going on such trips all over the world, especially to third world nations, had begun to invite him to go with them. Some of these trips were "fraught with danger," as these Americans, on more than one trip, smuggled Bibles in their luggage into China and met with house church leaders and members there, for example.

On other occasions my Dad would journey, like Paul the Apostle from Bible times, to other dangerous places where Dad on a number of occasions would issue an invitation and have 100-200 people raise their hands to receive Jesus Christ as Savior and Lord.

In fact, over a period of approximately 15 years, my father saw perhaps 20,000 men, women, boys and girls of all ages from all over the world take this step. This was especially true for those from lesser developed nations, where my Dad was able to pray with those people to receive Jesus as Savior and Lord and/or have prayer to receive healing. In these services my father was one of the featured speakers, or sometimes the only such speaker. Without a doubt, the Lord used Pastor Jim in a mighty movement of the Lord overseas during this time in his life.

During these years, my father would travel three or four times each year for periods of two to three weeks each time to 18 different Third World nations. However, these countries were not the ones someone would visit on purpose from the standpoint of being a great tourist destination. It wasn't Paris or Rome for a holiday, but Columbia, South America on numerous occasions to help bring about transformed lives in the people. Pastor Jim was understandably enthusiastic to be a part of what was taking place throughout Latin America and South America and many other places in the world, as more and more men, women, boys and girls of all ages accepted Jesus into their lives.

Indeed, Pastor Jim had and still has the heart of an evangelist. But, his circumstances changed one day when he came back from visiting his cardiologist/internist in St. Louis. At that checkup, his doctor simply told him that at nearly 78 years of age, he didn't think it was still appropriate to go on such trips because Dad had recently received food poisoning in his last trip. His doctor, Dr. Bill Phillips, simply didn't want something to happen in a country, where the medical care and facilities were sometimes "primitive" by U.S. standards. Mom seconded the motion and actually told my father that he needed to close that door so that the Lord could open a "new" door in the future for him. Her "suggestion" wasn't an easy one for pastor/evangelist/teacher Jim Armstrong to accept not only because it was what he had been doing since his official retirement 15 years earlier, but also because he had felt such a sense of fulfillment from doing it. However, he finally agreed, as the two of them prayed in agreement on releasing this assignment so that they could see what the Lord would do in Dad's life next.

But they didn't have to wait for very long. In fact, that night, an associate pastor of St. Louis Family Church, where my father and mother were members and which is perhaps the largest protestant church in St. Louis, called to bring up the idea of my father joining the church's staff full-time. In fact, he asked my Dad to pray about it and to discuss it with his wife. Next, the senior pastor (the church's CEO) of this 6,000+ member church, where the famous former St. Louis Rams quarterback Kurt Warner had once been a member, asked my father to get together for a meeting in his office to discuss the matter further.

The result was a full-time job offer to work as an associate pastor at St. Louis Family Church in Chesterfield, Missouri, which was followed by a modified acceptance. Mom voted "no" on any full-time job offer, which my father had emotionally wanted to accept. She had reasoned that such a pace might well kill my father. For his part, Dad finally agreed that while he might want to work that hard, perhaps, my mother had made a good point. So, he agreed on a 3-day per week modified job offer.

His primary assignment as associate pastor was to make "new" member calls, hospital calls and nursing home calls on church members, family members and their friends. Plus, Pastor Jim also began to teach a class on healing each day he worked on the staff, which was ideally suited to his past experience and background.

At age 78, he also learned for the first time to use a computer and to send and receive emails, for example, and to utilize the church's voicemail system. On hospital calls, Dad would speak words of life and encouragement to his "captive audience" in their hospital beds. Needless to say, many of those he visited, who had never before made professions of faith in Jesus Christ as Savior and Lord, would frequently do so after my father's visitation calls. In recent years, Pastor Jim Armstrong has become even more bold about his witnessing since he now sometimes includes room mates of these sick and recovering members, too, in his hospital room ministry calls.

Just before Pastor Jim turned 80, the same administrative pastor from this large St. Louis church once more asked Dad if he wouldn't like to consider coming onto the church staff full-time? Again, my father was interested. But, this time, on still another visit to his doctor, he complained about shortness of breath. His same doctor, Dr. Phillips, responded by ordering a heart-related test, which showed substantial blockage in a number of arteries leading into my father's heart. After seeing these test results, his doctor ordered an open-heart surgery, with five by-passes, for the following morning to repair the blockages. What was the result? A successful operation essentially gave Pastor Armstrong a "new heart" so he might actually live to be 95 or 100 years old. Perhaps, the Lord spared his life so that he could continue to be used to tell the Good News of Jesus Christ to a lost and dying world in need of a Savior.

Today, Pastor Jim long ago returned to work on a three day per week schedule, once again, and he is now 84 years old. In fact, recently, he told me that the church had expressed its appreciation, in part, by raising his salary from $10,000 per year originally to $27,000 per year today, despite his part-time status. Plus, he has a good attitude and he is glad to simply be alive. Of course, initially, he went to therapy; plus he takes medicine, which is not unusual for someone his age. In short, he still accomplishes much in all respects in his life.

But, the miracle in my father's life, which is such a great example for others, is that someone who is nearly 80 can still be offered a full-time job at all. And, while the conclusion might wind up being a part-time job for three days each week, instead of a full-time option, still the offer was extended to Pastor Jim Armstrong in the first place.

Finally, on the recent occasion of his 62nd wedding anniversary during a Friday evening service when Dad was taking my mother out to dinner, the senior pastor of his church announced that St. Louis Family Church was going to buy a "new" car for Dad as a much-needed gift and anyone who wanted to contribute was encouraged to do so. Surprisingly or perhaps not so surprisingly, over $20,000 was raised in just the first week toward the project. Soon after that, Mom and Dad were beginning their internet-based search for just the right car.

Chapter Thirteen

• Now What? •

Peter Quigley

**Entrepreneur/Media Innovator, Thought
Differently**

W hat was he going to do for the rest of his life or at
least during this next part of his professional,
working career? Peter Quigley, media executive
during his early 50s, was thinking these thoughts in 1998. Of
course, we often go back to one of our most fun experiences
or a particularly fulfilling part of our professional life, when
we begin to tackle such weighty issues relating to the next
phase. And, so too did Peter Quigley, the former Parade
Magazine senior vice president, who had actually increased
sales at Parade by $50 million just during 1st half, 1997 and
had also achieved a +50% profitability increase in the
process on that venerable publication.

For Quigley, his thoughts went back to his days of selling
and then managing as Vice President and General Business
Director of a significant, nationwide sales team at Media
Networks, Inc., which is currently a subsidiary of Time
Warner. This company was the one which pioneered the

sales of local full-page advertisements in major national magazine titles, which still include Time, Newsweek, US News, Sports Illustrated and such business management stalwarts as *BusinessWeek*, *Forbes* and *Fortune*, for example. In this instance, Peter actually managed 120 employees, including 70 domestic sales executives, 10 managers and a marketing staff of 12. Annual Publishers Information Bureau revenue of $75 million was generated in the process of selling 6,000 network insertions (30,000 ads) in the top 100 DMA metro markets on an annual basis.

With his background, Peter certainly realized that MNI's strength was in reaching men and especially those who were part of the professional/managerial class in our society. But, what about women? And, so, Quigley's thinking began to evolve. Didn't consumer spending account for 70% of the Gross Domestic Product? As a matter of fact, yes, that's right. And, didn't women actually account for 80% of all consumer purchases in America? Once again, right on, he thought!

Thus, Ad Ink Network was born, which initially was sold on a test market basis into just two metros in Boston and Detroit during the first year and with just one group of women's magazines from Hearst Publishing. In fact, Peter Quigley actually sold the first $500,000 in revenue himself and, in the process, achieved profitability during the first six months of his "new adventure."

So, what exactly does Peter Quigley and his sales staff of 50 or so independent media representatives do today? Collectively, they sell full-page, local advertisements in groups (called networks) of leading national magazines in the top 80 U.S. metro markets. This list of magazine stars includes the following: Good Housekeeping, Woman's Day and Redbook, plus Kiplinger's Personal Finance paired together with Smart Money in a somewhat smaller group of target markets plus Reader's Digest in Regional, State and Metro Editions. This custom magazine publishing insert business has grown from the ground up, as Peter has set up all the functions of the business, which have included sales, marketing, planning and forecasting, administration, manufacturing and financial management together with this list of exciting magazine publishers.

As a disclaimer, this writer also thinks highly of Peter Quigley and what he can accomplish in this venture in the future, as well as what he has already achieved in the past. In fact, this author previously served as Midwest Director of Business Development (i.e. sales manager) at Ad Ink Network.

On a personal note, Peter married his wife Margaret in September, 1978 and together they have a son John O'Brien Quigley, who is currently a junior in college in Illinois. As an aside, John also serves as the webmaster for the www.AdInkNetwork.com web site, which he designed. Also, interestingly, the Quigleys, who met during Peter's tour of duty with MNI in Detroit, were actually married by Peter's Uncle, Father John Quigley, who was then in charge of the Newman Center at the University of Massachusetts. But, because of a fire at their local Catholic church, they were actually physically married in a nearby Episcopal Church.

Recently, Peter Quigley and his wife Margaret moved into still another home in the suburbs of New York City, which they are restoring while living in the home itself. In the past, Margaret commented that this was one way for her to help the Quigleys make some additional money over the years. The couple has actually lived in a total of seven homes during their marriage.

Having grown up near Marblehead, Massachusetts, which is a northern suburb of Boston, Peter has long been an avid sailor, which he has often done with his wife and family. He also golfs, plays tennis and was a well-rounded athlete, both in high school and during college, Margaret commented. Quigley was even captain of his basketball team in high school, president of his class and a member of the National Honor Society in the Class of 1963. Plus, he was an enthusiastic lacrosse player in his younger days, too. Today, Peter listens to all sorts of music, reads books and of course magazines, even likes to cartoon a bit and often works seven days a week, which he definitely loves to do.

Quigley regularly attends a Catholic church near their home with his wife Margaret, who is a former security analyst and portfolio manager for a regional brokerage house prior to their marriage. Today, his wife serves as the Chief Financial Officer for their family-owned company, but she prefers the title of bookkeeper.

The exciting part about Peter Quigley's story relates to the possibility that an entrepreneur can still make it nationally in today's megamedia company environment, which has become increasingly dominated by some of the largest conglomerates in all of Corporate America. What's also exciting about Ad Ink Network is that in many instances it includes a group of senior media industry representatives, who clearly know what they're doing, but who would also be considered as retreads in an industry often dominated by young faces. Margaret described this part of their organization mission as "really rewarding both to Peter and also to me."

• Now What? •

Bob Robinson

Real Estate Developer, Turned to Sales

Most of us know of Donald Trump, the famous real estate developer. However, few of us probably realize that every part of the U.S., which is growing, has its own set of developers, who weather the good times and the not-so-good times to bring their real estate projects forward for the public to buy. Bob Robinson, until age 60, was such a man. But, today, he sells real estate for a major firm in the Northwest suburbs of Chicago, where he routinely adds a comfortable amount of additional income each year to his family's cash flow in the process. This is his story.

Bob Robinson was born in Crystal Lake, Illinois, a northwestern Chicago suburb, graduated from what used to be its only high school, where he played both football and basketball, spent most of his adult life there as a real estate developer in McHenry County (which includes Crystal Lake) and the surrounding area, and even today sells real estate to some of the many people he has known over the years in

Crystal Lake and its environs. Obviously, one of the keys to his sales success amounts to maintaining a large rolodex or, in today's parlance, a substantial database.

This author met Bob Robinson (a.k.a. "Slim") as a fellow member of the McHenry County College Fitness Center, where he and I often exercise at the same time in the morning 2 to 4 times each week. He often referred to me as "Hemmingway," even before he had seen any writing samples.

Bob Robinson (left) with author Jim Armstrong (right) at McHenry County College Fitness Center.

After graduating from high school, Robinson attended St. Ambrose College and then Beloit College. Because of his athletic abilities, he received a partial scholarship in both instances. Then, along came the Korean War, when Bob signed up to serve his country. Ultimately, he went through flight training and became an officer in the Air Force, where he served for a total of three years as a radar observer.

When his military tour of duty was over, he returned home and went into sales, at least initially with Proctor & Gamble, which was followed by a longer-term involvement with Ladd Enterprises, which was a residential home building firm. During the time he worked there, he ultimately became the Vice President of Sales & Marketing. Then, a stint in Florida was followed by a senior management position with United Development Corporation in Chicago, where Bob as President of the firm learned to play with "the big boys." At the end of that contract, he chose to go out on his own with a partner back in McHenry County, once again. That partner was Dave Ladd, who officed with Robinson in McHenry, Illinois.

But, at 60, Bob decided to retire because his finances were in good shape, which unfortunately cannot be said for many of us. However, over the next six months, he quickly began to miss the stimulation of working. So, Robinson changed direction and called on a friend, who headed up the local branch of Baird & Warner. In turn, his friend and business colleague was more than happy to agree to Bob's suggestion of joining his office. So, Robinson landed in a good spot nearly 13 years ago and he has been happy there ever since.

As a real estate sales agent today, Bob Robinson has joined the ranks of approximately one million men and women in America, who share similar duties and responsibilities. He chose Baird & Warner in the Chicago area because he always felt that this firm had the very best training program from his vantage point as a developer. In addition, with his sales, marketing and finance background, such a step represented quite a natural one for him to take. On a personal note, Robinson also wanted to stay busy and mentally alert.

In terms of his family, Bob Robinson and his wife have four grown children, including three boys and one girl. Interestingly, his oldest son Robbie, at age 51, works as a construction supervisor and himself lives in Crystal Lake. Bob's next oldest son Craig, at age 50, serves as vice president of operations of a Crystal Lake-based manufacturer. His third oldest son Jeff, who finished his degree and then went through evening classes to earn his MBA, now designs demonstration models for credit card holders at Discover. Finally, his daughter Lisa, who lives and works in Indianapolis, has been successfully engaged in the mortgage business in recent years.

For his part, Robinson still has fun; he likes to travel, plus he loves to interact with younger men and women who might be starting out in their career. He said younger men and women are full of life and optimism. Robinson and his wife Kristi, aged 60, travel plus they love to entertain.

On a personal note, Bob and his wife recently launched a cake baking company. His wife Kristi was doing well as a paralegal, who was working 2 to 3 days each week. But, at heart, she was a chef/baker, whose specialty was making a gourmet carrot cake. So, one day, she took a sample into a local gourmet store in Crystal Lake with the goal of selling some of her distinctive carrot cakes. The owner was impressed, ordered some of the great tasting cakes and his customers loved them too. Thus, Aunt Sophie's Carrot Cake was born.

In the meantime, Bob Robinson continues to sell real estate for Baird & Warner, still lives in his hometown of Crystal Lake, Illinois and he and his wife have fun every day. Plus, Bob gets to be married to "the Aunt Sophie," too.

• Now What? •

Chapter Fourteen

• Now What? •

Trends & Countertrends Examined

From the Heartland of America, economics takes on the familiar face of someone you know, who may have recently lost his/her job.

Should we blame the politicians in Washington, DC of this party or that? Probably not. On the other hand, should we blame members of organized labor or union bosses for asking for "too much" money? "No" because it's their job to at least ask the question. Or, perhaps, we may be tempted to blame senior management executives for their alleged "corporate greed." Once more, the answer comes back as "No" from analysts without "an ax to grind."

And, so, who is to blame, you might logically ask for the loss of so many manufacturing jobs in America during a time when most forecasters and government statisticians have said our economy is recovering? The real answer is the advent and increasingly rapid adoption of a global economy for our model, where everyone from all over the world becomes increasingly woven together. The short-term winners in this scenario become China, India and Mexico, in particular, in relationship to the loss of US manufacturing jobs due to an ever improving infrastructure in those countries plus cheap labor.

Never did this point become clearer than when a headline in The Financial Times, the global business and financial community newspaper, proclaimed that Levi's was ending its production in North America. And, yet, what could possibly be more American than a pair of blue jeans?

What are the politicians to do? The professional economic development community of city planners and vice presidents of Economic Development for regional chambers of all sizes in America have begun to mobilize. Yet, the answers are hard. Many people, frankly, do not want to have the questions asked, much less begin to listen to the solutions.

But, please understand this point. According to a 2004 Study from the AARP, 79% of our baby boom generation of men and women born between 1946 and 1964 currently expect to work in some type of capacity. However, approximately a quarter of the 77.5 million men and women who fall into this category, expect to do so because they think they'll need the money. Sometimes, there may not be any choice.

So, all of us need to be willing to demonstrate a greater degree of flexibility. Specifically, if we find ourselves out of a job in one place in America, we need to be prepared to move somewhere else, where jobs in our field/industry may be more plentiful. Also, we need to be willing to take advantage of state and county-sponsored job training programs. In this way, our basic skill set can be improved, which will also lead to a higher pay level, as well. We also need to consider going back to school, depending on our current age.

In addition, someone also needs to say loud and clear that there are already growing shortages of qualified workers to teach the children in our nation's schools. We are also beginning to experience nationwide shortages of nurses and pharmacists, as our baby-boom generation begins to retire.

Of course, you may have no interest in those options. And, so, please also understand that our nation's largest trucking companies are always looking for men and women, who are willing to be trained as drivers. While these jobs are difficult, they can also pay between $40,000 and $60,000 per year or more. For more information from a listing of major companies in the industry, please visit www.InboundLogistics.com. Our nation will also increasingly require workers at different skill levels to work in our distribution centers/warehouses. These jobs for unskilled labor will range in pay from $7/hour to approximately $20/hour, depending on the center's proximity to a major city.

Are there jobs in America? "Yes," but our attitude can and will make a huge difference. The old job models have changed at the same time many of us may still be clinging to those old ideas and attitudes about what constitutes work in America for blue-collar and white-collar employees alike.

Downsizing Hurts People

The appropriate word is "Ouch!" Invariably older employees are the ones being downsized or right-sized in Corporate America. Of course, all HR departments will deny the truth of this statement. But, I offer one simple question as a means of illustrating this most appropriate point. Specifically, when a downsizing formula is developed, how often is the winning formula some type of combination of years of service (which suggests an older employee) plus age (which again requires an older employee in order to max out on the formula)?

This writer has seen full retirement benefits provided for friends who are age 50 or 55 consistently on the basis of the use of this type of formula, which in some cases, can even be enhanced by the addition of additional years of age or service. This development suggests that younger and younger employees are taking advantage of such provisions for financial reasons. By younger on this point, I mean age 50 and over.

But, make no mistake about it: Age is the "key" factor involved in corporate reorganizations.

Healthcare Costs Are the Real Culprit

Have you asked one of your previously downsized friends how much he or she pays for healthcare lately? When the COBRA formula runs out after 18 months, you may be amazed to find out that a married couple in Illinois, for example, may pay $15,000/year for their coverage, assuming that there's nothing really wrong with them. In that event, the most economical health insurance providers will simply deny them coverage. Then, think about adding another, large chunk of money to that amount for coverage that employees previously took for granted at ridiculously low rates, which were even subsided by corporate America.

Here's a twist on the above formula. Have you met or talked with one of your friends lately, where his wife is actually working for 24 hours (i.e. 3 days) each week as a city librarian essentially because of the full-time employee status she gets, which then qualifies her to cover her family on a group health insurance basis for a "low cost?" A medical/dental/prescription drug benefit coverage on a low cost basis, without his or her spouse being disqualified due to some condition such as high blood pressure or diabetes, becomes a very tempting reason to take a lower-paying job for the benefit of your family.

The Medicare Gap Dilemma

If you're over age 50, how often have you had the conversation with more than one of your friends lately about getting to the age when your Medicare benefit will kick into gear so that you can then buy lower cost health insurance for your family? Between ages 55 and actual retirement, for example, this challenge alone can be daunting. Neither federal or state politicians have been able to develop pools of small businesses, with their employees, so that these companies could collectively aggregate to reasonably buy into such a group plan, except on a last resort basis at the state level. When someone leaves the employment of that large or mid-sized company or government job, for example, the days of excellent and inexpensive health insurance are over.

And, so, strategies for receiving lower cost health/dental/ prescription drug coverage during these "gap" years for you and your family becomes an important objective and necessity.

No one I know wants to run the risk of no insurance coverage in the meantime versus some type of unforeseeably expensive hospital stay for a family member. A no-insurance strategy for anyone with assets at all is simply not an option outside of a personal bankruptcy. Of course, that type of personal risk management represents no strategy at all.

The Self-Employment Model Gains Momentum Today

After being downsized a time or two, how many of your friends have now come to the same inevitable conclusion, regardless of where they live, regardless of their education level or occupational category and regardless of their gender or race? Plenty of them, according to my own experience in this area.

Just think about it. On the first day of your own business, you can get up and begin to wash your face or shave. As you do so, you should take a moment to stop and look at your best employee in the mirror. A suggested next statement from you might/should go as follows: "Jim, you're the very best employee I've got. And, I promise I will never fire you or downsize you from this company. Go get 'em, Tiger!"

Of course, while there are risks inherent in pursuing this type of vision, there are also obvious rewards, too. Many men and women, with long employment histories at some large company who then receive a large severance check as each one exits, will now wake up to the starting capital they require to pursue this dream. I have been blessed to meet a large number of men and women, who fall into exactly this category. This very circumstance may be precisely what you needed to take this step since the necessary capital is now available.

171

Future Labor Shortages Will Rule the Day

The best news for you as a 50+ year old is this: Because of the upcoming retirement of the largest age bloc in America, labor shortages will actually begin to develop in virtually every type of conceivable labor category there is in our country. This development, in the future, will benefit all employees/self-employed men and women in the labor market.

Increasingly, we will be able to work on terms, which will best suit us and our unique circumstances. We will be able to work part-time for three days each week, two days/week, three days each week on a 4 hour/day basis and many other versions thereof. We will also, in the future, be asked to continue to work past normal retirement age or we will be asked to continue working at "the company" as an independent contractor after our "official retirement."

The demand side of the labor equation will simply flip from employer to employee/independent contractor in the future. Otherwise, how will all of the work get done 10 years from now, for example? Just smile, as you think about this statement, because most of us, who are reading this prediction, will no doubt live to see this development take place. We will likely even be courted to continue working on some type of basis due to this upcoming labor shortage.

Companies may even develop some type of "special" benefit package for older employees and independent contractors.

Perseverance Today Will Pay Off Tomorrow

Despite the fact that today's situation may not look as bright as it will later, keep your head up, keep your attitude up, continue to make the calls and ask the questions; plus don't forget to pray to the Lord, in the process, also. And, remember "Never Give Up." That three-word summary of one of Winston Churchill's most famous speeches says a lot about our attitude.

Yes, we can choose to play the blame game of blaming someone else or "the company" or my unique circumstances or our parents or our wife/husband. But, at age 50+, my question to you, should you find yourself in the position of wanting to play this unfortunate game, "when do we actually grow up enough to take adult responsibility?" Hopefully, today is that day.

In addition, forgiveness is also the key to being able to move forward in the process of reinventing yourself after age 50. No one really wants to hear a long version of your story, even your spouse or significant other. By now, they have already heard it perhaps 50 times. Today, why not choose to simply give them a break from hearing it re-stated for the 51st time? It's your choice.

Just ask yourself: Would you really like someone else to tell you this story again, if you had to be on the "hearing" end of this equation? Today is also the day to begin to simply "get over it." Forgive and go forward. As a Christian, this point if actually a mandate stated as such in the Lord's Prayer. But, for others, in this reader audience, it still makes sense for you too, because it's common sense in terms of increasing your productivity sooner versus later.

Simply choose to make the effort to reinvent yourself today, regardless of why you are having to make such an effort. The "why" is much less important because it relates to your past. But, the point of this book more than anything else is to get to where you want to be for the rest of your working lifetime or during this next chapter of your life.

The choice is up to you. But, the time to begin to think differently, to act differently and to take steps leading to a different outcome for your life is NOW.

For more information about jobs from specific companies and other organizations, business opportunities and continuing education options, you are invited to visit the new web site for Baby Boomers and Active Seniors at **www.NowWhatJobs.net**.

You'll be glad you checked it out.

Lighthouse Publications · a light to the nations

Other Titles Available
from Lighthouse Publications

These and other Christian books from Lighthouse Publications are available at participating local Christian bookstores, Amazon.com & Bn.com.

To order books directly from Lighthouse Publications visit:
www.Lighthouse-Publications.com

Lighthouse Publications
2028 Larkin Avenue
Elgin, IL 60123
(847) 697-6788

Apostolic Team Ministry

Pastor/Prophet Scott Wallis provides practical answers to the questions that many believers have, such as: "How can I overcome lack in my life?" Learn why apostles are so important to the purpose and plans of God, and how apostolic teams release tremendous supernatural power and wealth into the Church.

Author: Scott Wallis
Retail Price: $11.99 (Paperbound)
ISBN: 0964221128

The Third Reformation is Coming

Prophetic leaders have been declaring for several years that a third reformational movement of the Holy Spirit was about to begin. Find out what this third reformation is and how it will radically change the Church and your life.

Author: Scott Wallis
Retail Price: $9.99 (Paperbound)
ISBN: 0964221144

How to Know if Your Prophecy is Really from God

One of the most important books on prophecy available for Believers. If you have ever received a prophetic word, then this book will help you discern if that word was from God, and if it was, what to do with it to see if fulfilled.

Author: Scott Wallis
Retail Price: $11.99 (Paperbound)
ISBN: 1931232415

Plugging into the Spirit of Prophecy

God has designed every believer to walk in the prophetic. You can learn how to flow in the Holy Spirit of prophecy. This exciting book will teach you how to do this and more. You will experience God's awesome power through the prophetic word.

Author: Scott Wallis
Retail Price: $11.99 (Paperbound)
ISBN: 1931232210

Entering the School of the Prophets

Scott Wallis's third book in his series on understanding prophetic ministry that answers questions regarding the prophetic office and its value to the Body of Christ today. A great resource for those desiring to understand more about the prophetic office and ministry.

Author: Scott Wallis
Retail Price: $12.99 (Paperbound)
ISBN: 1-933656-04-2

Decade of Destiny

A powerful prophetic word detailing what God is doing in our days. First written in 1991, this timeless book has proven to be an accurate window into the future. Discover what God is saying to His Church today!

Author: Scott Wallis
Retail Price: $11.99 (Paperbound)
ISBN: 0964221195

May I Please Speak with My Father?

A study resource, written to encourage women to pursue a deeper relationship with our Father. As you communicate with God and others through this book, it will bring healing and deliverance, allowing you to open your heart and share your own thoughts about both your earthly and Heavenly Father.

Author: Tanya G. Davis
Retail Price: $21.99 (Hardbound)
ISBN: 1933656026

Abraham: The Man, The Myth, The Legend

A fictional account of Abraham's early years, based in a Biblical worldview. All the wonder of God's redemption in the life of a young pagan man, his glorious romance with Sarai, the exciting action of battles and rescue encounters, and his discovery of the one true God of the universe.

Author: Imre Weinstein
Retail Price: $19.99
ISBN: 1933656018

Breaking Free from Destructive Relationships

Lynda Patrick explains the facets of spiritual control and abuse that so many believers face, giving insights into the beginnings and outcomes. She exposes the Jezebel spirit, and articulates the remedies that will "set free the mind and spirit...to the eternal purposes that were predetermined...before the abuse even took place."

Authors: Lynda L. Patrick
Retail Price: $14.99 (Paperbound)
ISBN: 193365600X

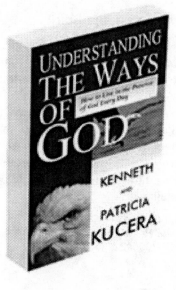

Understanding the Ways of God

You can understand the mysteries behind God's ways. No longer wonder why God does what He does – you can know. As you read this exciting book, you will learn secret after secret of walking in the ways of God. Unlock the potential God has placed inside of you as you learn the ways of God!

Authors: Kenneth & Patricia Kucera
Retail Price: $11.99 (Paperbound)
ISBN: 0964221152

The Message in the Miracles of Christ

Recently, some researchers have discovered that there may be hidden coded messages in the actual text of the Bible. Could it be that the miracles of Jesus also reveal hidden messages of what God is doing in our day? Discover the answer as you read this exciting book!

Author: Donna Carlisle
Retail Price: $14.99 (Paperbound)
ISBN: 0964221136

Growing in the Spirit

Taking from life examples, Pastor/Prophet Rudy Clark reveals principles of spiritual growth. Through many life lessons, God has taught Reverend Clark the values and virtues that have made him the man he is today. Experience freedom as you learn how to reach your fullest potential.

Author: Rudy H. Clark
Retail Price: $14.99 (Paperbound)
ISBN: 0964221160

2010

LaVergne, TN USA
12 December 2010
208454LV00003B/112/A